Connecting
Across
Cultures

Connecting across Cultures

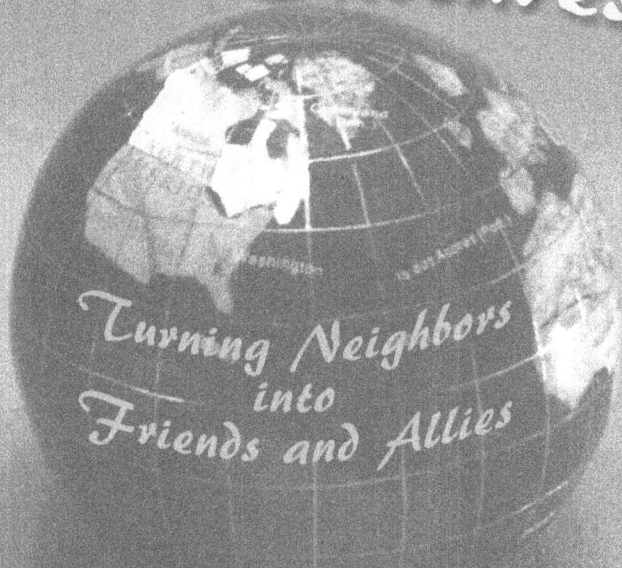

Turning Neighbors into Friends and Allies

Carol Paradise Decker

SUNSTONE
PRESS

SANTA FE

Sunstone books may be purchased for educational, business, or sales promotional use.
For information please write: Special Markets Department, Sunstone Press,
P.O. Box 2321, Santa Fe, New Mexico 87504-2321.

Book and cover design › Vicki Ahl
Body typeface › Laurentian Std
Printed on acid-free paper
∞
eBook 978-1-61139-335-4

Library of Congress Cataloging-in-Publication Data

Decker, Carol Paradise, 1927-
   Connecting across cultures : turning neighbors into friends and allies / by Carol
Paradise Decker.
      pages cm
   ISBN 978-1-63293-034-7 (softcover : alk. paper)
   1. Multiculturalism. 2. Culture. 3. Interpersonal relations. 4. Multicultural-
ism--New Mexico. 5. New Mexico--Social life and customs. I. Title.
   HM1271.D44 2014
   305.8--dc23
                           2014036241

WWW.SUNSTONEPRESS.COM
SUNSTONE PRESS / POST OFFICE BOX 2321 / SANTA FE, NM 87504-2321 /USA
(505) 988-4418 / ORDERS ONLY (800) 243-5644 / FAX (505) 988-1025

*T*his book is dedicated , with appreciation, to all *vecinos* of whatever varieties who are working to improve communications and relationships in their respective multicultural communities.

Contents

.

About This Book

Is it about Santa Fe, New Mexico, in the 1990s?
Yes. That's where it all began.
Is it about the people who live in this multicultural area?
Yes, and how they get along.
That's race and culture, problem areas.
It doesn't have to sound so divisive.
Then it's about relationships?
Yes, and how to make them better.

I hope the experiences described here will help you cope with increasingly multicultural populations in your community, wherever you may be.

A Word About Santa Fe
La Villa Real de la Santa Fe de San Francisco de Asis
(Yes, really, this is the official name for our city)

It was founded in the early 1600s as the capital of *Las Provincias Internas* of the Spanish Colonial province of New Spain (Mexico). It was built on the remains of an abandoned pueblo in this beautiful valley bounded by the Sangre de Cristo Mountains on the east and the Jemez range to the west. The settlers, landholders, ranchers and missionaries quickly spread throughout what is now Northern New Mexico.

The "Spaniards" were not all white-skinned Europeans who actually came from Spain. Many were *mestizos* with various mixtures of Spanish and Indian blood. Others were Mexican Indians, particularly Tlaxcalans, who came as servants and helpers in the heavy work of constructing the community and farming the land. New Mexico was a long way from the cities and resources of the south: trains of heavy freight wagons periodically lumbered across the deserts and rough country bringing supplies the colonists could not make themselves. The journey took about six months. Few women came with the settlers; so liaisons with Pueblo women were common, producing the next generations of sturdy, brown-skinned New Mexicans

Many pueblos, ancient communities of Indian farmers—the name in Spanish simply means "villages"—sprinkled the area, particularly along the Rio Grande. Franciscan missionaries came to "save the souls of the poor, heathen Indians," and to make them "contributing vassals of the Spanish Empire." The Pueblo people provided labor and tribute to their overlords and helped construct the mission churches that arose in every pueblo.

The Pueblo Revolt in 1680 drove out the Spanish settlers for twelve years. After their return, led by Don Diego de Vargas, Spanish oppression eased and alliances formed, Indians and Spaniards joining forces for survival in this harsh land.

In the 1800s, the Anglo invasions began. They swarmed in, especially after the Mexican War when the United States annexed the northern half of the Republic of Mexico in 1848. Great changes followed. A new language superseded the common Spanish. New laws conflicted with traditional Spanish legal patterns. New religions arrived and the familiar local Catholicism was revamped along French practices. New customs and values often conflicted with what the people had known for generations. Racism and exploitation followed, as did Anglo contempt for the "little brown people" and for the treaties enacted in good faith. Though many of these changes were good and necessary, the resulting cultural conflicts still affect our communities today.

Today, tourist brochures celebrate the tri-cultures of New Mexico, where Indians, Hispanics and Anglos live together in apparent harmony. After all, we have Indian and Hispanic markets that show and sell the best of traditional and contemporary arts that bring thousands of visitors to Santa Fe. Museums and galleries promote their arts along with those of the burgeoning Anglo community. Restaurants serve up the tastiest of local ethnic dishes. Music and dances on the Plaza, and in the Pueblos, fiestas and countless smaller events bring people together. All our cultures are richly and frequently displayed for all to see and appreciate. And truly, it is a rich place.

But that's only surface veneer. New Mexico stands almost last in national statistics about education, alcoholism, drugs, violence, school dropouts, teen pregnancies, incarceration, abandonment, and a whole range of additional social problems.

Why? Theories abound. Read on.

✥ *1* ✥

An Introduction

A transplanted Yankee, I came from Connecticut with my retired husband in 1980. For years, I had been teaching Conversational Spanish and Hispanic Heritage to adults and working in various intercultural situations. Here, I continued teaching Spanish; and as I explored New Mexico, I wondered how I could help bring people together across the cultural gaps I was seeing.

What a lot I had—and still have—to learn.

For eight years, mostly in the 1990s, I developed an organization we called *Vecinos Del Norte.* Doesn't *Vecinos* mean "neighbors"? What's the difference?

Well, according to the dictionary, both words refer to someone who lives near you. But the Spanish word goes farther than the English one. *Vecinos* implies not only someone who lives near you but also someone with whom you have a relationship. It's someone with whom you talk, share, celebrate, combine resources, build alliances for your mutual benefit. It's a caring, supportive connectedness that goes beyond the geographical implications of the English word at a time when "neighbors" barely notice each other.

Here in Northern New Mexico, people of many cultures live side by side, as neighbors. Yet, with happy and notable exceptions, most of us do not relate comfortably with neighbors of other backgrounds. We are separated by history and heritage, by our values and ways of doing things, by our experiences and language—even when we are speaking English.

Although some people are comfortable with their cultural identity, many others feel confused, besieged, angry. Some are eager to reach out to others across the cultural gaps; many others become anxious, defensive, insensitive. For many of us intercultural relationships seem threatening because they challenge us to look at our own values and lifeways from different perspectives. For others, these same relationships are welcome as a way of expanding knowledge of human experience, including our own.

Northern New Mexico, as in many other parts of the United States, has been changing rapidly over the past few years. New residents are swarming in; developers are overbuilding on huge tracts of ancestral land; prices are spiraling upward beyond the reach of local people; TV, computers, electronic gadgets and economic pressures are threatening old values. As people are displaced and traditional cultures eroded, a seething undercurrent of anger, despair, defensiveness and frustration exacerbates the "ethnic tensions" that in some areas threaten to explode in violence.

This undercurrent of intercultural distrust is real and growing. Things haven't changed much in the years since *Vecinos* started in the 1990s. Yet the problems we face—education, employment, justice, violence, exploitation, abuse, dropouts, to name just a few—affect ALL of us. These problems should bring us together across the cultures as we attempt to resolve them to our mutual satisfaction.

It's too common and easy to insist that one thing is "an Anglo problem," or that something else is a "Hispanic concern," or that another issue is "for the Indians to deal with." It takes energy, sensitivity and commitment to see that we are all involved and needed for creative solutions to complex problems.

But we don't know how to talk with each other across the cultures. We don't know how to build trust, to listen to each other's concerns to develop cross-cultural relationships that will not only enrich our own perspectives, but also help us become allies in our battles for common goals.

It was hard to describe what *Vecinos* was trying to do. One attempt went like this:

> *Vecinos Del Norte* has been bringing people together across the cultural lines to explore and celebrate our respective heritages, to consider current issues, to build personal relationships and to help us all in working together for our common future as more sensitive and caring neighbors and *Vecinos*.

How were we trying to do all this?

We hosted many informal *conversaciones* with resource people from various backgrounds, people involved with their Indian, Hispanic or Anglo communities, people working in cultural preservation or intercultural affairs. There were lots of them who were eager to share their perspectives—if asked. Word of mouth, flyers and notices in the newspaper brought in interested participants who contributed their own concerns and insights to the general discussion. We videotaped many, edited them down to half-hour programs, and showed them weekly on Public Access TV.

We made field trips to Indian Pueblos, to Hispanic villages, to schools and clinics and to community centers; and we hosted potlucks in return. We visited potters, weavers, saint-makers, churches, small businesses and more, and everywhere received warm welcomes. We joined work projects, plastered old adobe churches, cleaned up after a fire, loaned our assistance and technical know-how to many struggling groups. Panel discussions were lively, with varying viewpoints illuminating current situations. Workshops helped us consider such things as breaking stereotypes, listening and conflict resolution. Small group discussions that "just happened" around cups of coffee and cake were often intense. Personal invitations to Pueblo dances or Hispanic fiestas enriched our experiences. Many of the contacts we made have lasted for years.

We shared our developing perspectives through newspaper columns, through the videotapes already mentioned, through flyers and small brochures, through three years of *A Directory of Intercultural Resources* (and there were lots of them), and through frequent talks in churches and community groups.

Who were the "we" I refer to here? "We" were mostly Anglos but with large numbers of Hispanics, Indians and others joining us frequently. We had contacts and welcomes all over the north, from Cochiti Pueblo to Tierra Amarilla. Well over a thousand participants were actually involved in one way or another, and the spin-off spun far. Some events brought out only half a dozen participants, while others filled a meeting room with eighty or a hundred. Everything was volunteer, nobody was paid for anything. Donations covered our basic expenses of postage and printing. I was general creator and coordinator with substantial assistance from a varying group of helpers. Borrowed spaces in churches, schools and homes were our meeting places, and the telephone our major communications link. The numbers of events we hosted were staggering. Eventually, exhaustion and politics closed us down.

The results? Well, I can't say we changed the intercultural climate of the community very much, but we raised some important questions, suggested some possible solutions, and for many participants of all backgrounds we provided rich, perspective-changing experiences.

When we began the project, I consulted with several local Hispanic leaders. Each one exclaimed in amazement, "What's going on here? When you Anglos want to learn about us, you go down to the University of New Mexico to the professors with fancy PhDs who have studied us and are the experts. But you are asking US for OUR knowledge and experience! This is something new!"

This book is dedicated, in a spirit of gratitude, to all who have participated in *Vecinos* events, and to those who have shared their perspectives and experience, their homes and work places, their stories and laughter, to help us build a more sensitive community.

So, Reader, sit back and consider with us some of what we were hearing and learning through our *Vecinos* experiences. Perhaps some things will be useful to you in your own intercultural contacts.

But this is a handbook, a workbook, and invites you to respond to the various situations described here. Argue, fight, cheer, jeer, celebrate. Make this your book as well as mine.

❖ ❖ ❖

On the following pages, I'll share with you some of the lessons our *Vecinos* experiences taught us about "crossing the cultures." Though it's written from an Anglo perspective, many of them should be useful to people from other cultures too.

The themes I tackle are crucial. They include: the power of names, the tri-cultural trap, culture and cultures, stereotypes, heritage, values, racism, communications, conflict, bridges—and more. All of these themes must be considered as we interrelate. And though the focus is on relationships, the implication is that these relationships will lead to action and alliances as we work together on community and individuals' problems.

Somebody commented that "nobody knows how to create a true intercultural community here in New Mexico. It has never been done. We're constantly experimenting, exploring, trying out ways that may, or may not, work out." *Vecinos* is one of these experiments.

Some of this text is "commentary," by me and others, introducing a theme or reflecting on some of its manifestations. Illustrative stories are sometimes included to add to the account.

A large part is *Vecinos' Voices*, quotations more or less intact, by individuals that reveal perspectives on some of the larger issues we're dealing with. *Vecinos* is committed to listening to people as well as to academics and "experts." Though there are plenty of resources—books, documentaries, articles, films—they must not substitute for contact with real people.

Vecinos Vistas are situations either observed by me or reported by reliable informants. Some of them are informative or infuriating, others are challenging and invite your response. What would you do or say in a situation like this?

Included also are many helpful tips about dealing with cross-cultural contacts. These are summarized and expanded in the last chapter.

May these pages help increase your awareness, comfort and effectiveness in your intercultural associations, and lead to warm, enriching friendships for many years.

Vecinos Has Taught Us That:

There are many amazing people of all cultures "out there," who are living creative lives within and for their respective communities, who have welcomed us and shared richly with *Vecinos* participants.

There are also many problems "out there," with much pain, anger, frustration, tensions and anxieties about cultural/economic/community survival, both within and among the various cultural groups. Listening makes these problems understandable, and sometimes suggests appropriate resources that might help.

Stereotypes abound, cutting in every direction. "Generalities" may be a useful shorthand (i.e. Indian, Hispanic, Anglo), but within each group is incredible diversity. Stereotypes cause us to see only what's expected, often making "invisible" the real people involved. And stereotypes often hurt!

Heritage must not be ignored. The cultural/historical and personal experiences of today's ethnic groups and individuals are essential parts of how and why we function today. Anglos usually have short historical memories. Those whose ancestors have been here for generations typically have long ones. Ignore them at our peril!

Cultural values often clash. There are too many examples to elaborate here, but values are hard to talk about because they generally lie beneath the surface of our consciousness, deeply embedded in the emotions. We need to learn to talk about these, and to respect them, whether or not we agree.

Cross-cultural communications are complex. They include not only words, which often have different resonances across the cultures, but also body language, expectations, time and space elements, past experiences and more. Listening to each other on many levels is essential, and can be learned.

There are different cultural ways of getting things done. Task-oriented, efficient Anglos normally have quite different practices than relationship-oriented others. The individual initiative prized by Anglos is often in conflict with community-oriented leadership styles. More papers (like this one) and business meetings often intimidate people who process information and make decisions in different ways. We need to be sensitive to things like these.

Cultural timeframes are different too. Anglos often want instant results, friendships, relationships, trust. But usually for Indians and Hispanics, these things develop slowly. Planning for the immediate "now" often conflicts with the sense of stable heritage and concern for the distant future—the "seven generations" some have told us about.

Racism, real or perceived, by whatever name, is a fact of life for a large portion of the people here, both Native and Anglo. Almost everybody has stories to tell. For some people they are discouragements, for others they are a spur to accomplishment.

Living in two worlds is hard work. Those Indians and Hispanics who work in the "dominant" Anglo world, where values, obligations and lifeways often conflict with much that is taught in their own culture, don't have a lot of extra energy, or interest for Anglo-style meetings or concerns. Raising their kids to function in multiple worlds provides many dilemmas, as it does for Anglos, too, in this rapidly changing, consumer-oriented "dominant" culture surrounding us.

Someone described the "parallel cultures" of New Mexico, which are mostly self-contained and interact only around the edges. Yet these "edges" can be places of conflict or caring cooperation. It depends on us.

All of these things, and more, need to be considered as we reach out to build intercultural relationships. There are many people, books, videos, exhibits, experiences, opportunities that can help us all learn. And most of us need to learn more about our own culture, as well as those of others.

Reaching out across the cultures is both challenging and enriching and takes a lot more time than we expect. And it can be scary for all parties concerned. But people everywhere respond to a smile and an outstretched hand, and a willingness to listen and share. As we help each other, we can laugh at our mistakes, grow in our confidence and rejoice in developing friendships.

At this time, as always, our community needs *Vecinos* of every heritage who can help build bridges across the cultural gaps so we can work together more effectively for our common future. The challenges are enormous. The opportunities are rich and varied. The task is vital for our mutual survival.

Some Perspectives

"I used to wish that all those other people would simply go away, disappear. They, mostly Anglos, caused so much stress and conflict among my own

Hispanic family, in almost every aspect of life, that I wanted to eliminate all of them. It was especially bad when we considered issues like land and water, language and culture, economic and cultural opportunities. My family has lived here in New Mexico for many generations, and they feel strongly about these things.

"Then one day I had a revelation. It was, simply, that these "other people," whatever their heritage, were not going to go away! They were here to stay! And instead of spending so much energy trying to make them disappear, maybe I should figure out how to get along with them more effectively. That began a whole new focus for my work, in helping people to communicate more clearly across the cultures, to work together, to see each other as allies confronting the challenges that affect us all."

—Roberto Chene

Southwest Center for Cross Cultural Relationships, Albuquerque, New Mexico

❖ ❖ ❖

"Why do we so often think of intercultural relations as more of a problem than as an inspiration. We can learn so much from each other about the complex business of living our lives, consider alternative solutions to thorny situations, deepen and enrich perspectives on our own cultures and values. There are some amazing people "out there" working on creative approaches to conditions we know little about who deserve our respect. It's a pleasure and inspiration to know such people and to be able to work with them on mutual concerns.

"This in no way minimizes some of the very real conflicts "out there," but maybe gives us tools for seeking answers together."

—Carol

Vecinos Voices: Sample Comments Heard Around My Neighborhood
(*How would you respond to these comments?*)

"Intercultural relations? Why bother? This is an Anglo town now. If those Hispanic folks can't adapt, that's tough. As for the Indians, they bring in the tourists. Otherwise, send them back to their pueblos. A bilingual state, so mandated by the Constitution, you say? Phooey! English is where it's at, everything else is irrelevant."

—(A brusque Anglo)

❖❖❖

"I can help you with that problem! We had a similar situation in Boston, and this is how we solved it."

—(A well-meaning Anglo)

❖❖❖

"No, I don't want to meet him. He's a Mexican. He gives me the creeps. His dark skin is disgusting, and I can't understand what he says. He acts suspicious and I want to call the police."

—(A European lady, newcomer, about a neighbor)

❖❖❖

"I know they're out there, like coyotes, but they don't have anything to do with me. I'm busy. My life is full with job and family and friends and so many things in Santa Fe to enjoy. I don't have time to take on any Indians, and I'm not much interested in them anyway."

—(An Anglo neighbor)

❖❖❖

"I do so want to learn about the people of New Mexico, particularly the Indians and Hispanics. I've studied Anthropology and the history of these people, and I'm eager to make friends with some real live ones. How do you think I should start?"

—(An eager newcomer)

❖❖❖

"I was beaten in school if I spoke Spanish and the only thing I learned about my people was that Coronado came and was bad to the Indians. I grew up feeling bad about myself and my people."

—(A Hispanic neighbor)

❖❖❖

"I never thought much about Indians until I was walking past a booth

at Indian Market. A young woman was selling a pot to a customer and I over-heard her say, 'I'm going to Harvard . . .' I only heard a bit of the conversation, but my ears pricked up. What a surprise! I had never thought of Indians as people before, going to elite universities and studying—what?"
—(A long-time Anglo resident)

❖❖❖

"Anglos? They've taken over our town, they and their money. They and the changes they've brought in. They don't care what they do, what they de-stroy. They don't pay any attention to us, they act as if we're irrelevant. Maybe we are."
—(A local Hispanic)

❖❖❖

"Indians? They like our money. They bring in the tourists. They go back to their pueblos. They're not really part of Santa Fe."
—(A rich Anglo businessman)

❖❖❖

"Anglos? We like their money. Otherwise they can go away and leave us alone."
—(A visiting Pueblo Indian)

❖❖❖

"Those White kids dump trash all over the place and their parents blame US! Not fair!"
—(Hispanic high school student)

❖❖❖

"If you want someone to do a job for you, call a Mexican. They work hard and well, I've always been pleased with them. But the local Hispanics? No way. They'd rather live off the government dole. They don't like to work, particularly for us Anglos."
—(A local Anglo)

❖❖❖

"NOT FAIR!"
—(A Hispanic student working three jobs.)

"I LIKE those people across the street! They're Hispanic, warm and welcoming. They invite me to their family parties. What a lot of folks come to them! Big ones, little ones, all ages. I can't begin to keep track of everybody. Lots of interesting conversation. I listen and learn a lot. And there's so much good food! I wish I could do more in return."
—(A lonely, retired Anglo widow)

From An Early Flyer

"*Vecinos* means "neighbors" in the special sense of people who relate to each other and care about each other, as well as live together in the same areas.

"*Vecinos Del Norte*, based in Santa Fe, reaches out to people of many backgrounds and cultures throughout Northern New Mexico.

"*Vecinos Del Norte*

Brings people together across the cultures
   to TALK with each other,
        to work and to play,
           to build relationships:
to SHARE and to CELEBRATE
   our respective heritages;
to LEARN about current issues;
to EXPLORE the creativity
   and the challenges
        of changing cultures in collision;
to FIGHT racism, prejudice,
   stereotypes,
        misunderstandings
           and the gaps that often separate us;
to HELP us work together more effectively

for our common future;
and to BUILD together a caring
multicultural COMMUNITY
with appreciation
and opportunities for us all."

❖ *2* ❖

What's On a Name?

What do other people call you?
What do you call yourself?
Why does it matter?
What does it tell about you?

Names?

Let's look at names for a bit. Though often taken for granted, they are a clue to our identity and cultural orientation.

Given by our parents (Susan, Jose, Barrack), affirmed by our families (Jones, Sanchez, Nakamura), often linked to our heritage (Miller, Garibaldi, Lomahaftewa), or places of origin (Griego, Deutsch, Szpakowski), they set us firmly within a community and an inherited culture. Names changed at marriage link us to other families or communities, whether in the Spanish style of family inclusions (Elena Maria—baptismal name, Robledo—father's name, Sisnero—mother's father's name, de Romero—husband's father's name), or in the modern patterns of hyphens (David Baines-Sawyer—wife's name added). Embellished with titles (Doctor, Reverend, General) or eradicated (Prisoner No. 12345), they are sources of identity, pride or disgrace. Even bland names (John Smith, Mary Brown) tell us something about the recipient.

Our names can be an inspiration or a burden, or something we never think about. It's easy to change them, either legally or casually, for one that better represents who we think we are. Despair at a family heritage (slave owners, exploiters, welfare cheaters) can lead us to affiliate with a different image. (My then four-year-old grandson, the youngest of three, insisted we call him "Batman" or "Luke Skywalker" for the power and authority reflected in those figures.)

Would you respond differently to someone named Adams? Dumbrowski? Garibaldi? Toya? Smith? Red Cloud? O'Hara? Trujillo? Khalsa? Powers? Sze? Many people would. Such names may lead to stereotypes, which can confuse communications and cause unnecessary tensions.

Names often reflect culture, which is open to affirmation or abuse. Depending on context and intentions, they can be friendly or hateful. Who is calling who "Nigger? Wetbacks? Redskin? Queer? Gringo? Bodies and souls have been damaged, lives have been lost, as such terms, voiced by hostiles, batter undeserving individuals. Yet the same terms in other situations can be considered endearments.

What do we call ourselves? Why does it matter? With who or what do we identify? Consider the following "Voices."

Names For Every Occasion

Names, as labels, are inevitable. As sources of identity, often wrong, they can cause discomfort, pride, laughter or indignation. Depending on the context, they can be hurled as insults, offered with respect or even tendered with affection. Here is an assortment of comments about the power of names:

"What did we call ourselves before Columbus came? That's a question often asked. And the thing is, in every single tribe, even today, when you translate the word we each had for ourselves, without knowledge of each other, it was always something that translated to basically the same thing. The people. The human beings. That's what we called ourselves. And we still do."
—A visiting Indian elder

❖❖❖

"As for me, Carol, I'm proud to be a New England Yankee. It explains much of who and what I am, and provides a special energy for all I do. But I suspect that my interpretation of Yankee is misunderstood by most people who have different stereotypes of what a Yankee ought to be."
—ME

❖❖❖

"I'm proud to be Chicano. It gives me my sense of who I am, of connectedness to my people, of a goal and direction for my life. I can hold my head up in any situation wherever I am."

—A warm and effective community leader

❖❖❖

"Gee! I'm just what I am. You can call me Bob."

—A young Anglo

❖❖❖

"My Mexican friends call me la *gringa* or *gringuita*. It's okay. They are friendly. It's much easier to say *gringa* than *estadosunidense*."

—An Anglo student

❖❖❖

"I'm Texan, born and bred. But I guess I have to prove myself here. I understand that Texans are not particularly popular in some parts of Santa Fe. But why?"

—An anxious visitor

❖❖❖

"I'm Hopi. My mother told me never to respond if people call me an Indian. I'm Hopi, and that's something special."

—A young, lovely teacher

❖❖❖

"I hear you don't like to be called Anglos, even less do you like the term Gringos. Now John Wayne used to call White people "Pilgrims." All White people like John Wayne, don't you? Why don't you try that term for a while. You might like it, Pilgrims."

—A Cochiti Indian to a group of Anglo tourists

❖❖❖

"Don't call me a Native American. That's just a bureaucratic word, made up by the BIA. It's demeaning. I'm an American Indian, a Sioux. Better still, just call me a human being."

—An Indian Activist

❖❖❖

"They call me a Hispanic, but I don't really know what that means. My family has been here in New Mexico for a long time, but I'm just an ordinary American girl. Just because my name is Romero, I guess that labels me in a way I don't understand."

—An attractive young woman

❖❖❖

"I'm an American, a New Yorker. Now I'm here in New Mexico. That's all we need to know."

—A newcomer to New Mexico

❖❖❖

"When young people ask me what I am, I tell them, 'I'm an Indian, a Comanche. And what are YOU?' Most of them seem confused by the question, wishing they knew, wishing they could say with pride and clarity what they are…"

—A veteran teacher

❖❖❖

"People of Color! That's the silliest and most patronizing term I have heard. I know the speaker tries not to offend, but he offends ME. After all, I change my color with the seasons and often I'm more brown than some of the 'people of color' I know. It sounds as if it's bad to be pale-skinned, and it lumps us all in a colorless stereotype. I tell you, it's okay to be White or whatever shade you are, but 'people of color'? Yuk!

—An annoyed White man

❖❖❖

"We never considered ourselves as Americans. *Los Americanos* were the enemy the oppressors, the robbers of our lands, our culture, our livelihoods. I work in the Americano world now, but I've never felt quite comfortable in it. I'm an old-fashioned Hispano, and proud of it.

—A creative, successful businessman

❖❖❖

"Don't call me Chicano. I don't go in for all that political stuff. I'm a peaceful, traditional Spanish-American. I don't want to make waves. My life is good as it is."

—A cheerful shopkeeper

❖❖❖

Meet Pedro

He was mad at the world, but he wasn't exactly sure why. Was it because of his brown skin? Or his poor English? His poverty? His resistance to the education taught by his Anglo teachers? The scrapes he got himself into? The way people called him *Mexicano* as a term of contempt? He lashed out at everybody, earned a reputation as a bully and troublemaker; and he spent time in prison.

He went to Washington and joined the Poor People's March.

Walking along beside him was a little old white-haired Anglo lady. "What's your name?" she asked him.

"Peter," he responded.

She looked him over. "No, I don't believe it. Tell me, what's your real name?"

Again, "It's Peter," he insisted.

A few minutes later she asked him again. And finally he burst out with, "Okay, it's Pedro!"

The little old lady was delighted. She hugged him and exclaimed, "Now you know who you really are!"

She started telling him about some of the historic Mexican leaders and how they had influenced their people. Pedro was amazed. He had never heard about such leaders, nor anything good about Mexico.

Now "Pedro," when he went home, thought deeply about what she had told him. He started reading about Mexican and New Mexican history and began to look at his community with new eyes. How could he help his people? he wondered. Teach them about their heritage! Improve medical care! Fight off exploiters who wanted to develop the land! Preserve the traditional values of the Hispanic people!

He was still mad, but now he knew why and had a creative focus for his anger.

—As told by Pedro himself

The Tri-Cultural Trap

"Santa Fe, the tri-cultural city different where Indians, Hispanics and Anglos all live together in peace and harmony." So say the tourist brochures and promotional information. It's a great oversimplification, and not entirely true. Let's take a look.

Our Tri-Cultural Trap

Many cities across the country have large immigrant populations and vibrant intercultural communities that deal with their joys and problems each in its own way.

But Santa Fe, "The City Different," is dealing with intercultural tensions that date back generations. Of course, visitors and residents can visit the Pueblos and Hispanic villages, go to museums and countless events that celebrate and interpret the cultures involved. They can find living communities that perpetuate many of the old customs. It's like walking into a time machine. But we don't necessarily notice the tensions. We see what we want to see.

Those who look more deeply can see that each community is struggling, in its own ways, to embrace the future while honoring the past. It's not easy.

Our tri-cultural emphasis attracts visitors. Much of the local economy is based on this. Yet most visitors and many of the residents are quite confused about who makes up these three cultures.

Thumbnail sketches of the main categories follow, with more detailed descriptions later.

Why do I call our three-culture description a "trap"? Because it pushes us all into categories that lead to simplistic stereotypes that blind us to the true diversity of New Mexico. Yet for the sake of convenience I'll continue to refer to our Indians, Hispanics and Anglos as background, as jumping-off places for further exploration. Join me.

New Mexico Indians

Pueblo People, many of whom still live in their nineteen ancestral villages along the Rio Grande and its tributaries. Their traditions, rituals and languages are still vital, and as sovereign nations each has its own elected government. Some of their people are well-known potters, jewelers and artists of many descriptions. Many sell their crafts in front of the Palace of the Governors, huddling in the winter cold or broiling in the summer heat. Others are educated professionals working in the area, or employees of various businesses. Some tend tribal ventures of their pueblos, from teaching to farming to casinos. Others find relationships with the Outside World too difficult and barricade themselves in the safety of their individual pueblos. Substance abuse and domestic violence are troubling issues all the tribes are struggling with, and many innovative programs have sprung up in response. On Pueblo feast days respectful visitors are welcome to see the traditional dances, many of which go back hundreds of years.

The Navajos prefer to live in isolated family groups spread out over the vast colorful desert landscape to the west, though some are moving into towns closer to human services. They once were feared warriors and raiders, attacking Pueblo and Hispanic ranches and settlements, carrying off captives and livestock. Now they tend to be shepherds, weavers of handsome rugs and silversmiths. The Navajo code talkers during the Second World War are still honored, and many young men choose the military. Tony Hillerman's novels are a good introduction to Navajo life.

The Hopi are related to the Pueblo people, live on mesas surrounded by Navajo land, farm the dry desert as they have for centuries, and their wise men have a reputation for holiness. Most people have to go elsewhere for work.

Apaches live on two reservations, the Mescaleros at the south, the

Jicarillas to the northwest. Once the scourge of the settlements, now they tend to be ranchers and livestock tenders. The Mescalero have gone into the hospitality business, have a large guest ranch—The Inn of the Mountain Gods—and a ski resort.

The Institute Of American Indian Arts (IAIA) brings to Santa Fe Indians from tribes all over the country, as students and teachers, for long and short periods of time. They have a huge new campus south of town, and a museum opposite the Cathedral.

The annual Indian Market each August attracts hundreds of Indians from all across the country to show and sell their products, and thousands of buyers to purchase them. It's a huge event that takes over the Plaza and most of the downtown with artistic and educational spin-offs that enrich the whole community.

Hispanic People

Most *Nuevo Mexicanos* can trace their families back to the early settlers some three or four hundred years ago. They, too, were a hodgepodge of races and origins, some from Spain and other parts of Europe, others from Mexico or mixtures of Spanish and Indian blood. New Mexico, as a province of Colonial Spain, was always isolated by distance from "mainstream" Mexico, even more so after the American takeover in 1848. Dominated by American laws, exploiters and an alien culture, the old customs and values were disparaged, the traditions diminishing. Though the young no longer speak Spanish and most know little about their heritage, a special warm flavor permeates the Hispanic presence. But there is still much prejudice against them in many areas, leaving suppressed anger under the surface. This needs to be recognized so it can be dealt with.

Mexicans are also Hispanics, though they are different. There are thousands of them here in New Mexico. Many are long-term legal residents, citizens with families and businesses and a role in the community. Others, refugees from poverty and violence, have arrived here more recently. They struggle for survival, with or without documents. As with most immigrants, they come with a certain energy and optimism, eager to build a new life for themselves and their families. And others come for temporary jobs so they can send money back to their relatives in Mexico. But they generally scorn the New Mexican "Spanish Americans," who talk funny, think funny, don't even speak proper Spanish, and seem shy when confronted with Mexican energies. They don't relate, and sometimes tensions erupt.

Central Americans are another part of the Hispanic mix. From Guatemala, El Salvador, Nicaragua, they have fled civil wars, political oppression and environmental disasters. They bring their crafts, skills and good humor, but since few of them speak English they are mostly confined to menial jobs in restaurants and the like.

So you see, the Hispanic scene is rich and complex.

And The Anglos

As for the Anglos, they are everybody else. We come from everywhere with energy and desire for change that's intimidating. With short historical memories, it's the present that matters. By fair means or foul we try to take over a place regardless of the traditional inhabitants. The rich people build mansions on hilltops; the thriving middleclass has made Santa Fe a lively "destination community" for visitors; "New Agers" have made this a mecca for alternative healing; while sports enthusiasts flock to the mountains. We support museums, opera, concerts, educational institutions, fiestas, arts of many kinds, international venues and so much more. "Anglos" include Tibetans, Jews, Blacks, Germans, French, Chinese, Vietnamese, Irish, Italians, Pakistanis, India Indians, and everything else you can think of. We have made Santa Fe a wonderfully diverse community.

But most of us have very little knowledge or sensitivity to the traditional inhabitants of the land, and therein lie the sources of many of our problems.

And...

I haven't yet introduced the Mixtures. They are part of the complexity here. It is said that every Pueblo family has some Spanish blood and every Hispanic family is part Indian. As people travel around so much, many in the military, to many parts of the world, spouses from many backgrounds become part of our wonderful, crazy, mixed-up community.

New Mexicans and Americans

Mexicans—Indians—Spanish language—Primitive superstitions—Catholic—Papists—Ignorant peasants—Devilish ceremonies—Lazy, lethargic—Dirty—No 'git up and git'—No yen for progress—Ignorant—Backwards—Brown skins—Red skins—Not worth much.

From the 1850s through the 1950s—and even sometimes today—these attributes were despised by the Anglo establishment and most of its people. The Americans had won the War with Mexico and annexed the whole northern part of that country. The New Mexicans were a "conquered people" and were treated as such. The Indian Wars were still going on (until the 1880s) and Indians were feared. (See" The Black Legend" in chapter 6.)

Ignorant of American ways, the New Mexicans were ripe for exploitation, and exploiters swarmed in from the east. The Treaty of Guadalupe Hidalgo, guaranteeing rights to land and culture, meant nothing to the Anglos and everything to the New Mexicans. Read the history books and listen to people. Their stories are vivid, about broken treaties, illegal land grabs, confusing legal systems—in many cultural and economic ways the Anglo juggernaut rolled over the New Mexican people, leaving pain and anger that still simmers below the surface.

The United States was faced with an enormous challenge. How to incorporate this vast territory into its mainstream; how to bring modern resources to ancient cultures; how to assimilate Native people who didn't want to be assimilated, especially in the face of so much prejudice against them. Many efforts were benign, fostered by honorable and well-meaning people. Others were not. Resistance then, and sometimes even now, has marked each step along the way.

The American invasion has brought innumerable blessings to all New Mexicans. But it is very difficult for most of us Anglos to recognize past (and present) abuses that have left an underlying anger, a victim mentality, and often downright discrimination against the Native people. Just listen. They'll tell you.

Indian and Hispanic people are now seen as glamorous, exotic, tragic, picturesque, with their arts and ancient customs, bringing in the tourists and their dollars. Is that another form of exploitation? Tri-cultural New Mexico, come and see!

On The Other Hand...

Much of Northern New Mexico as we know it now is the product of the artist colonies of Taos and Santa Fe over the first half of the 1900s.

Some of the artists came for health reasons (Santa Fe sanatoria tended many tuberculosis patients, lots of creative people among them), some for adventure (the "Wild West" was still "wooly"), some to escape the restrictions of Eastern society. They fell in love with the landscapes and the Native people. The difference they made was profound.

This was the era of "Lo, the poor Indian!" and "The only good Indian is a dead one" and "Let them all die off and our Indian problem will be solved." And the Hispanics—Spanish Americans—were not much better off.

The artists, on the other hand, saw Native people as people. They painted them with dignity and respect. Their pictures spread far and wide as the Santa Fe Railroad reproduced them in promotional posters and calendars. It was the first time that many people had really looked at an Indian or Hispanic person. The artists celebrated the Native crafts, the pottery, weavings, woodcarvings; they found ways to improve their quality and marketed them all across the country. They established schools and training centers for the arts and crafts. They painted huge murals in public places to display the drama and beauty of the Pueblo-Hispanic experience. They helped preserve land and traditions, revived moribund festivals (like Santa Fe Fiesta) and created new ones (Zozobra). They rescued the Pueblos from certain disaster, as in the Bursum Bill (see chapter 8). They encouraged their economic successes. They brought in tourists to visit Pueblos and Hispanic villages in conjunction with the railroad and Harvey House Hotels and tours. They launched fine museums and arts markets. And they became friends, supporters and allies.

They also channeled them according to their own romantic vision. Here was the "noble red man," the ancient people living the traditions of their ancestors, simple people with deep spiritual roots connected with the natural world, Hispanics with the blood of the *conquistadores* surging through their veins. They were peaceful, creative, friendly people who welcomed visitors, and the artists wanted to keep them that way.

They did an amazing job of celebrating, saving and promoting the Native people, laying the groundwork for today and especially for the "tri-cultural" community we see now. But whatever did not fit in their romantic molds was ignored. (What do we expect, for Pete's sake, they were ARTISTS!) But many of the things they ignored are the roots of persistent problems of the present.

Vecinos Voices . . . Tri-Cultural Trap

"I hate this tri-cultural thing. It keeps us from seeing the wonderful diversity of our New Mexican people. For instance, are you aware of the many racial/ethnic strands that came here from Spain alone? Redheads, blondes from North Europe, dark-skinned Mediterranean types, Moors from North Africa, folks with Jewish blood and practices, Blacks . . . Add the Indian blood from Mexico and the local pueblos, and the French and Anglo blood mixed in, and we have a very complex set of people called 'Hispanic.' Tri-cultures? Phooey!"
—Orlando Romero, historian

"What's an Indian, anyway? Last I heard, if you're one-eighth Indian by blood and registered with a recognized tribe, you're considered an Indian. But it keeps changing and varies from tribe to tribe. There are lots of wannabes fighting for looser definitions. There's money in it."

—A puzzled Anglo official

❖ ❖ ❖

"What a surprise for a Jewish boy like me. Here they officially consider me an Anglo! This is a land of enchantment! I called my father a couple of nights ago and told him that now that we're Anglos, maybe he can join that restrictive golf club he was interested in."

—Laughing Jewish historian

❖ ❖ ❖

"Hey! I'm just an ordinary American girl. I go to high school. I get As in many of my classes. I play in the band. I have lots of friends and life is good. My folks, they're old fashioned. They say they're Hispanic, but that doesn't mean much to me. Their parents didn't even speak English! I had nothing to do with them."

—A young neighbor

❖ ❖ ❖

"Look at me! I'm Black! Don't ever call me an Anglo. That robs me of my heritage and all I've accomplished in this life. I've come a long way and made it in a demanding Anglo world where my people are few. I'm proud of what I've accomplished. Just don't call me an Anglo!"

—Retired educator

❖ ❖ ❖

"My family is a real rainbow family. Lots of my brothers joined the military and brought back spouses from overseas. Hawaii. Vietnam. Italy. Germany. They've all brought something special to our New Mexican Hispanic roots and we've welcomed them all into the family. But what do we call us?"

—local Hispanic

❖ ❖ ❖

"Call me Hispanic? No way! These "Spanish Americans" you have here have nothing to do with me. I'm Mexican, and proud of it. I'm not part of your three cultures."

—A Mexican resident

❖❖❖

"Where do I fit in?"

—A lonely Tibetan

❖❖❖

"Who cares? What's that got to do with anything? Basketball's where it's at. We play every day after school. Sure, we're all colors and shades. But all that matters is how well we play the game. Our backgrounds are irrelevant, we live in the now. Go away and don't bother me with your questions."

—High school student

❖❖❖

"Those tourists over there, they're really something! They wouldn't believe I'm an Indian because I don't wear feathers and I speak good English. I told them I don't scalp people, either, but sometimes I'm tempted. A friend wanted to bring in some turkey feathers to put in our hair and a drum and we'd do a war dance all around the Plaza. The tourists would love it, their stereotypes would be confirmed, and our sales would soar. But then we decided it would be too disrespectful and we forgot about it. It would have been fun, though."

—A Pueblo vendor on the Plaza

❖❖❖

"I don't know what I am. Actually, I'm a bit of everything. I was the only White Protestant kid growing up in a small New Mexican town. I played with the Hispanic kids, spoke Spanish, went to the Catholic Church and to school with them. I identified with my Hispanic friends as well as with my Anglo family. Later I worked with various New Mexican Indian people and was adopted by a Navajo family, so I have a deep love and sympathy with them. I guess that makes me just a New Mexican . . ."

—Community worker

A Note:

On these pages I will continue to use the terms "Indian"–"Hispanic"–"Anglo." Each represents multiple strands of complex cultural backgrounds and of current realities. Each is made up of infinite numbers of individuals.

I am not using these words as stereotypes, but as shorthand terms of convenience.

Clarification: The *Vecinos* "Voices" and "Vistas" reflect the experiences and perspectives of certain individuals and in no way represent the whole situation being considered. *Vecinos* is committed to listening to ordinary people as well as to "academics," and individuals have many diverse reactions to their heritage and surroundings.

For any mistakes, misinterpretations, or misquotes, I am solely responsible.

✤   *4*   ✤

Of Culture and Cultures

"*W*e like to think of ourselves as competent people. And generally, in our own culture we ARE competent people. But everything is different when we enter another culture. We don't know the "rules" and for a while we don't feel competent at all. It's not a good feeling."

—Dr. Edward T. Hall, Cultural Anthropologist, at a *Vecinos* meeting

Too often we think of "culture" as a refined taste in the arts—literature, classical music, sculpture, ballet and the like. A "cultured person" delights in art shows, the opera, and theater for instance.

"Culture" as we're using it here refers to the totality of life patterns, inherited, adopted, or absorbed through our heritage. An Englishman, for example, is very different from an Arab. An Argentinean has little in common with an Eskimo. Likewise, Anglo perceptions of the world and our place in it have little relationship with the Indo/Hispanic patterns of New Mexico.

Part of each culture is visible in arts, music, clothing, food, families. But the greater part is below the surface, barely recognized even by its members until challenged. It involves underlying values, how things have always been done, attitudes and authority.

Look at the chart on the next page. As you think about it, make one that represents your own culture, with specifics, as much as you can.

Cultures are like rafts floating around in a pond. People can float on these rafts all their lives, happy and secure as long as they stay in the middle. The problems begin when the rafts bump into each other, compete for space or for the fish in the pond, when their people see what other rafts contain or intend, when they want bigger and more luxurious rafts for their own people.

Each sees different aspects of the pond, with various ideas about solutions to its problems and about celebrations to unite the varied riders on the rafts. With communication and cooperation, together they could make the pond a rich and sustaining environment for ALL their people.

Of course, there are many sub-cultures among the major traditions we are talking about. The "tips" on these pages should help relate to most of them. But for now, let's focus on the principal cultures under discussion.

Some Aspects Of Cultures Are Obvious, Visible. Most other aspects are below our level of awareness, until challenged.

Some Examples

Visible Aspects:

Food—Language—Families—Literature—Music—Arts—Religion—Clothing—Games—Cooking—Celebrations—Dancing—Achievements—Skin color—Ornaments—Sports—Careers.

Less Visible Aspects:

Attitudes toward Authority—Environment—Clocktime—Leadership—Courtship—Death/Dying—Education—Personal Independence—Success—Women—Physical Space—Justice—Relationships—Problem Solving—Spirituality—Accomplishments—Sex—Kids—Old Folks—Communications—Emotions—Words—Cleanliness—Individuality—Heritage—Privacy—Status—Work—Tradition—Land—Water—Worldview—Bug Words—Alcohol—Racism—Generations—Generosity—History—Natural World—Knowledge—Wisdom.

These aspects vary with the culture and the person, but need to be considered in cross-cultural—and human—relationships.

Some Basics

It's important to remember that most immigrants to America (excluding slaves) came voluntarily to escape oppression or hardship, to find freedom and a more hopeful future, and to shape their lives in new ways. Their families, within a couple of generations, eagerly blend into the culture of their adopted home.

But that's not true for the Indian and Hispanic people of the American Southwest. Deeply rooted to the past, they cherish their heritage of centuries, especially when under pressure from the "dominant" American culture. To "blend" means to lose their identity, the traditions that make them who they are, and the values cherished for generations. Stories of pain, dislocation, prejudice and racism (brown skins!) circulate at every family gathering. Resistance and rage are often near the surface, erupting in some of the social problems we see every day.

The question is this: how can the heritage of both our Indian and Hispanic neighbors become a nurturing force as we all move into the future? Some people are working on this! Let's help them.

Cultures are not static. Like everything else, they change and evolve. Sometimes it's due to internal pressures or new leadership. Sometimes to external factors like contact with other cultures, or with new technologies, or broader education that invites new thinking. Normally there's a push-and-pull relationship between traditional practices and new visions. The process can be painful as conflicts split communities and families, or it can be a process eased by mutual respect. A "lost" culture, destroyed by outside forces, means "lost" individuals, searching for a positive sense of self and a solid place to stand.

The modern era seems to be sweeping everything away in front of it. Much that it brings is good and useful. But HOW can we, of all cultures, recognize and preserve the values that have made us human in our different ways? Read on!

Danger And Opportunity

Cultural diversity brings both danger and opportunity. Danger that we will split into warring factions, undermining and seeking to destroy each other. Danger of cultural separatism that fails to recognize the validity of others. Danger of cultural isolation that limits our approach to problems that afflict us all

Opportunity to learn from each other about the complex business of living, of being human in our world at this time. Opportunity to hear alternative perspectives to help us formulate our own. Opportunity to make the systems of our society more responsive to the needs of all its people.

Some people approach intercultural contacts with interest and enthusiasm, ready to learn, to share, to interrelate. Others find cross-cultural contacts frightening, and are hindered by shyness, prejudice, anxieties. Most of us are somewhere in between, and vary from day to day.

The following tips may help to ease or deepen cultural relationships for New Mexicans of all backgrounds.

A smile, a greeting, an outstretched hand are good beginnings. A sense that we see each other as people and are not looking through each other as symbols or stereotypes. A friendly comment about the situation that brings us together, a quip or a question. Person to person, relationships can happen.

We're guests—or hosts—with people from another culture. Rules and expectations are unfamiliar. We must mind our manners, go slow, treat people with courtesy, caring and respect. Remember, the other person may feel as shy—or even terrified—with us as we are with them.

We need to listen more and talk less. Words, chatter, questions, opinions can make the air so busy that we can learn little and communicate badly. We need to use our eyes and ears and other senses more effectively, and to appreciate the context as well as the people.

Humor and a light touch are essential! Can we laugh at our inevitable mistakes? Can we enjoy sharing "fun" things—food and play, music and jokes—across the cultural lines? Even serious matters can be dealt with in a humane way.

Degrees of Cultural Comfort

This is a complex issue that affects most of us at one time or another. For most of us it changes often, depending on many factors. Sometimes we respond with enthusiasm and energy to intercultural situations; sometimes we retreat and avoid the same. Where would you be today in regard to these questions?

With which kinds of people are you usually most comfortable? Why?
Which kinds of people do you tend to avoid? Why?
Do you look at individuals rather than cultural types? Why?
What value do you see in noting the heritage of the people you meet? Why?
Do questions like these seem to you irrelevant, insulting, phony? Why?

Most of us at different times and places go through a wide range of the following symptoms. For YOU, what kinds of conditions influence your reactions? None are "right" or "wrong." They just "are."

On the following list, where do you place yourself today?

You Have:

____ Mild discomfort with people whose language, looks and customs are different from your own. You limit contacts, avoid when possible.

____ Extreme discomfort. You avoid, stereotype, tell jokes to hide discomfort.

____ Panic! You try to escape. You share disparaging stories about such people.

____ Indifference, have little contact with cultural others, not much interested.

___ Comfort with all sorts of people regardless of their heritage.

___ You have an intellectual interest only, lots of academic information, but you bog down with personal relationships.

___ You are mildly curious about other "lifeways," but "spectatoritis" is enough.

___ You depend on stereotypes, both positive and negative, with little effort to look at the "realities."

___ You romanticize people of other cultures. "Lo, the poor Indian!"

___ You are delighted with cultural differences, see strength and relevance in cultural diversity.

___ You are angry at past and present injustices, real or imagined, by people of one culture toward another.

___ You are ethnocentric: Your way of thinking and doing things is the right one, all others are inferior, backward, wrong.

___ You like or dislike individuals because of who they are regardless of cultural backgrounds.

___ You are comfortable with your own heritage/culture, are willing to listen and learn from others.

___ You are uncomfortable with your own heritage, eager to embrace others in search of "truth."

___ You think you have come to a good balance, of respect for the realities of your own culture and openness to the experiences of others.

✣ *5* ✣

Neighbors

*H*ere's a closer look at the traditional cultures that share the "Land of Enchantment" as the tourist brochures call New Mexico: the Indians, Hispanics, and Anglos.

Though Indians of many tribes live and work in Northern New Mexico, let's focus on our Pueblo Neighbors.

Many newcomers to New Mexico are surprised to learn that the nineteen Rio Grande Pueblos are not all alike. Each Pueblo is distinct with its own language *(there are five different linguistic groups within which there are numerous dialects),* its own government, traditions and religious practices. Though nominally Catholic, their ancient traditions are strong. Most visible to outsiders are the seasonal dances that sometimes involve the whole community. These are not "entertainment" but serious rituals honoring the spirits and the creatures of the natural world, and they must be observed with respect.

Over the generations, many situations have threatened their lands and cultures, though these were guaranteed to them by the Treaty of Guadalupe Hidalgo in 1848. (See notes on the Bursum Bill in chapter 8.) As a result, they have "hunkered down" protectively within their tribal communities. Although many work in the mainstream world, there's a pervasive distrust of outsiders who "may be out to get them," based on generations of experience. Their basic values often conflict with those of the surrounding Anglo culture, which makes adjusting to the two worldviews difficult. Warm friendships can develop with caring outsiders: anger is generally directed at systems rather than individuals.

Each Pueblo is recognized by the federal government as a sovereign nation, responsible for its own affairs. Relationships can get sticky when they deal with state and federal issues, particularly around land and water, businesses and jobs, jurisdictions and laws. On January 6, most of the Pueblos change their leaders, transferring the traditional canes of authority to the new governor and his staff. Consistency can be a problem as the new officials may have different perspectives from their predecessors.

The Pueblos are cohesive communities, authoritarian in style, with strong claims on their members, including those who live elsewhere. Many of their people are doing well—economically, artistically, professionally. But many others are not. Poverty, violence and abuses of many kinds are pervasive. Tradition is strong in all the pueblos. Yet new or renewed projects are sprouting everywhere.

Most of the Pueblos have their own elementary schools and send many of their young for secondary Indian-focused junior and senior high education to the Santa Fe Indian School, which is sponsored by the All Indian Pueblo Council. Income from the many casinos helps support social services. Head Start, senior centers, upgraded clinics and community centers are some of the beneficiaries. Some projects focus on heritage, renewing the vitality of ancient traditions; while others refurbish arts and agriculture, Native languages, storytelling; or they teach computers, nutrition, farming and more. There's a lot going on if you care to look.

Occasional victories on the national scale raise spirits everywhere. For instance, the repatriation of remains of some two thousand ancestors that had been excavated by archaeologists in the early twentieth century and stored at Harvard University were returned for reburial at the once great Pecos Pueblo in 1999. This event brought out hundreds of their descendants to celebrate the occasion. This was the result of the government program NAGPRA (Native American Graves Protections and Repatriation Act) that mandates return of human remains and sacred objects from universities and museums to Native communities that want them.

The Pueblos have survived for centuries and will continue to do so on their own terms. Though they relate to the wider communities around them, they don't blend and shouldn't be expected to do so.

Pueblo People: Voices And Vistas

Lunching with an Indian friend, I asked him casually what he thought about the Bering Strait theory that his ancestors had walked across the land bridge from Asia to populate the New World.

He laughed. "Well, we think it's the other way around. Our ancestors were created here first, and they migrated the other way, across the land bridge to populate Asia. That's the way we see it."

My eyebrows went up in surprise. Did he really think that? Science tells us differently. Was he teasing me? I couldn't tell. But what did I know?

❖❖❖

Two Indian women, both innovative educators, were riding with me from one of the mountain villages to their Pueblo in the valley below. The Hispanic family and friends who were launching a new community center had invited our *Vecinos* group—about twenty people—for a festive lunch today with music, conversation, warm hospitality, and lots of good food. The happy vibes lingered.

One of the women said sadly, "Our families used to have such rich friendships with people in these mountain villages. But no more. The old relationships are lost and gone. Maybe, with your *Vecinos* help, we can reconnect again. Today was a good start.

The other was looking at the splendid view of the valley ahead where the lowering sun picked out the shapes and colors of the landscape. "Look at all these colors! I had forgotten. They used to look all gray."

"What do you mean, all gray?" I asked.

She hesitated a bit, then, prodded by her friend, explained. "We used to be drunk all the time. We simply couldn't see the colors. But now that we've stopped drinking, the whole world looks brighter, so beautiful! We have something important to do with our lives now, so we don't have to drink."

❖❖❖

"How can I hire these Indian guys?" lamented a local businessman.

"They are good workers, competent and willing, pleasant fellows. But their loyalty is to their pueblos. They constantly have to go back there, sometimes for days at a time, with no warning, to take part in dances or other Pueblo affairs. That's often when I need them most. I can't use such erratic employees. Sorry."

❖ ❖ ❖

The theme of the evening was Indian realities. One of our speakers, familiar with what's happening all over the Indian world, had given an optimistic account about how tribes are finding their voices, initiating businesses, demanding political recognition, educating young and old. A young man stood up, one of the students from IAIA. For a few minutes he just stood there, silent, until all eyes were upon him. Then he identified himself as Mandan/Hidatsa and began to recite a list of names. Slowly, solemnly, names and ages. Young people. We wondered what he was trying to tell us. Twenty or more names, while nobody moved.

Finally, he addressed the speaker. "These are the names of relatives and close friends who have died of violence or suicide over the past year. What do you say to that, Mister Speaker?"

The room remained silent. The speaker, obviously moved, didn't have much to say. Finally, he mumbled something such as, we still have much work to do, and the meeting broke up soon afterwards.

It was an unforgettable moment.

❖ ❖ ❖

The five kids in the park were obstreperous, acting like the 'wild Indians' I presumed they were. The young Indian woman with them seemed exhausted. I spoke with her in sympathy. She explained, 'These kids are not all mine. I'm tending some of them for a few days until their mother gets out of the hospital. Her man beat her up again. She always goes back to him. I don't know why. Meanwhile, I'm stuck with her kids as well as my own. Costs money.'

Just then, the ice cream truck came by. I bought ice cream for all of them. I don't know why, except that it felt good.

❖❖❖

Regarding creation stories, one Indian friend told me:

"When Mother Earth was creating human people, she shaped them out of clay and baked them. The first batch she took out of the oven too soon and the figures were pale, white, undercooked. They were you White people. The second batch she left in the oven loo long. They burned, came out all black. Those are the Black people and there aren't many of them here. But the third batch came out perfectly, with a lovely, soft, red-brown color, crisp and tasty and beautiful. That's us, we Indians. We're just right!"

❖❖❖

My friend was agitated. For many years, he has worked with Indian people. When I met him in the street, he grabbed my shoulder.

"Do you know what these hotel people and tour leaders are doing? They're sending their clients over to the Pueblos on their feast days, assuring them that they can get a free meal in an Indian home. They barge into open doors. That's an abuse of hospitality! People, friends are invited into pueblo homes and to share the festival meal. Their hosts will never turn away any strangers, even though the swarms of outsiders appearing at their doors can seriously strain the family resources. The women spend all week cooking and baking and buying stuff, and sometimes they feed as many as 200 people—in shifts, of course. Though most of them are poor, a major part of the Pueblo culture is sharing what they have, even if it ruins them. Children are taught to give, rather than get presents. How can we teach people to treat our Pueblo friends with respect? We can't let the tourists exploit them this way!"

❖❖❖

A Pueblo boy of 16 or 17 was part of a panel of youngsters preparing for a trip to Russia. The other students and most of the audience were Anglo. The topic of humor came up.

"What do Pueblo people laugh at?" someone asked.

The boy's eyes lit up, a grin split his face, but he quickly sobered. "I can't tell you," he insisted. But under pressure he finally conceded, "We laugh at YOU. You White people. The things you say and do, and your total ignorance, strike us as very funny, and there are more of you every day."

"Can you give us some examples?" someone asked.

"No way," he responded. "You wouldn't understand them."

This brought a storm of delighted laughter from the White people present, who thought his remarks were pretty funny, too.

❖ ❖ ❖

A young teacher, new to a pueblo school, wanted some advice.

"My second graders already want to know why they have to learn all this 'Anglo stuff.' They insist it doesn't have anything to do with them. They're proud of being Indian and that's all that matters to them. What can I tell them?"

❖ ❖ ❖

A couple, new to New Mexico, described their confusion on their first visit to a Pueblo feast day. They were standing quietly under some trees waiting for the dances to begin, trying to remain inconspicuous.

"He gave us those big loaves of bread, and here we were standing there feeling like idiots, not knowing what we were supposed to do about it."

A little old man, a red bandanna around his white hair, his face all wrinkly, had emerged from a nearby house carrying two large, round loaves of bread fresh out of the outdoor clay oven, the *horno*. The visitors wondered where he was going with them and were astonished when he stopped in front of them and thrust the loaves into their hands.

"We've heard how desperately poor these people are and we didn't want to take anything from them. We were also a bit afraid of being exploited in some way we couldn't anticipate. And so we stuttered and stammered, 'No thanks . . . we don't need any . . . give it to someone else,' and finally, 'Can we pay you for this? How much do we owe?' But the man, his face wrinkled up in a friendly smile, simply turned around and went back to his house. What was going on here, and why?"

❖ ❖ ❖

At San Ildefonso one day, I overheard three women chatting in a combination of their own Tewa and English.

One sighed and said in English. "I do so envy those people out at Jemez Pueblo!"

Curious, I asked the obvious. "Why?"

"Because nobody else speaks their language."

"So?"

"Their religious secrets are safe. Nobody else can steal them. That would destroy their power."

Nuevo Mexicanos (New Mexican Hispanics)

*Familias Y Fe (*Families And Faith). These are the bedrocks that have sustained the New Mexican Hispanic culture over the generations. They give meaning, value and continuity to every phase of life. They unite the people in strong webs of relationships, caring and love.

These and chile: Red chile . . . Green chile . . . Christmas Chile . . . Spicy . . . Hot . . . Tasty . . . Delicious—Breakfast . . . Lunch . . . Dinner, embedded in our culture. We take some when we travel. What would we do without it?

Families: Big ones. Extended. Multigenerational. Those who have gone before are not forgotten, and are still present in spirit. Relatives of every age and condition living nearby, in constant contact. A warm, loving nest where youngsters find caring, security, and experience the progression of life from birth to death. A nest that is hard to leave, and that calls back the ones who have flown away. A caring community within the larger communities of church, city and state, where each person has value to give and receive.

Families are also controlling. They can shape the future of the young by subtle and obvious pressures. The family is what is important, not the desires of individuals. Authority comes from the top down. The old folks are cared for as long as they live: their dictates and their blessings influence all decisions. When a family member leaves the area, he ruptures the fabric of the family.

Higher education can be a threat because it takes people away. When one is in trouble, the others leap to defense. Babies are welcome. . . . Families are what you can count on.

Faith: Catholic faith is all pervasive. Familiar adobe churches. Masses. Ancient Liturgies. Choirs and Mariachi Masses. First Communions. Baptisms and Funerals. Rosaries. All the ancient rituals that unite people in the faith. Saints. Celebrations. Joyful Processions. Posadas. Penitentes. Lay Ministries. Soup kitchens. Care for the poor and suffering as the faithful reach out into the world. Eucharistic Ministers. Mystics. Miracles. Holy People. Visions that attest to the realities of the Unseen. Pueblo Eagle Dancers in churches at Christmas. Participation is woven into the fabric of every day, every season, every family life.

Family and Faith make a rich mix, an alternative reality quite incomprehensible to secular, individualistic Anglos.

But Hispanic memories are long. Past abuses rankle, as do prejudice and discrimination that they still encounter from the intrusion of the Anglo world.

Hispanic *Voices*

"We never considered ourselves "Americanos" when I was growing up. They were "the Other." They had the power to hurt us. At school they beat us for speaking our own language and told us that Coronado came and was bad to the Indians. And that we should be grateful to the Americans who came to rescue us, but from what I wasn't sure. We didn't know any of them personally, and didn't want to . . ."
—Hispanic friend

❖ ❖ ❖

"My grandmother was wonderfully skilled with a needle. I remember watching her create beautiful things, tablecloths, bedspreads, scarves, with designs and little animals and flowers embroidered in colorful patterns. I could never do that. Though she tried to teach me, my fingers were too clumsy. But what she was most proud of was the clothing she made for La Conquistadora, the ancient wooden statue of the Virgin in the Cathedral. What colorful materials, what elegant designs, what fine stitchery! She loved to dress the statue in her many fine outfits and get her ready for the processions. The Caballeros de Vargas, with their red cummerbunds, carry her on a litter through the streets while the bells in the Cathedral peal merrily and little girls strew flowers in her path and people from all the parishes, carrying banners, join the procession. It meant a lot to her, as well as it does to the rest of us."

—Hispanic woman

❖❖❖

"Family? Mine have been here in New Mexico since 1630. We're all over the northern part of the state. I'm constantly running into relatives I didn't know I had, and connections that surprise me. Tracing our families back as far as we can along with all the ramifications is a favorite pastime. We're good guys and bad guys, rich folks and paupers, skilled craftspeople and politicians, farmers and fighters, priests and sinners, all of us interesting. Families occasionally get everybody together for a barbecue or a matanza and there are hundreds of us."

—Hispanic friend

❖❖❖

"Las Posadas? It's my favorite time of year. For nine nights before Christmas groups of us go around from house to house. The old Spanish song asks for shelter for Jose y Maria. The people outside the house sing one verse, the people inside sing another refusing help and telling the strangers to go away. Finally a door opens, the people inside sing songs of welcome, and everybody goes in for a party. We used to do this every year with friends from the church, but now my daughter makes fun of it, says we're stupid and old fashioned and she would rather watch her TV. It hurts."

—Local friend

❖❖❖

"We used to go out to the small town where my grandparents lived, the whole crowd of us gathering there. Their children, grandchildren, uncles and aunts, in-laws, friends and who knows who else. There must have been more than a hundred of us, of all ages, some of us rich and successful, some of us barely scraping by. We'd start out doing chores, painting, repairing, cleaning up the land, scrubbing the house inside and out. But first we'd greet the abuelos, and, kneeling, receive their blessings. Later there'd be a mass or rosary or prayers of some sort reminding us of what's important. And then the feast with many people contributing all the old dishes and the chile and the wonderful smells pervading the atmosphere. Plenty of time for talk, for admiring the babies and catching up on all the news. Everybody had stories, particularly the abuelos with their memories of times gone by, and we settled down to listen and to share.

"Then somebody would bring out a guitar or an accordion and the old songs reverberated around the vigas or the campfire. One old uncle usually brought out a bottle of his hooch, and we'd start feeling pretty mellow until the fights began. That was enough. Our sweet little abuelita, the granny who cared for each of us, was a tough cookie. She broke up the fights and sent us all home.

"Since the old folks died, we don't go there any more. But we gather our own kids, their spouses and children and their friends whenever we can. You're welcome to join us."
—Hispanic neighbor

❖❖❖

"Unless you have worked the land, loved it and raised crops on it with your own sweat and muscle, you can't really understand the lives and feelings of your Indian and Hispanic neighbors."
—Hispanic urbanite

❖❖❖

"Of course, I'm a Catholic. I was born one and I'll die one. It's important to me. I believe in God, but I don't go to church. I don't like those priests telling us what to do."
—Hispanic friend

❖❖❖

"I spent a student year in Mexico. I expected other people with Hispanic background would welcome me, like cousins. But I found, to my disappointment, that my classmates spurned me as just another gringa. So I suppose that we New Mexicans are something special, with our own heritage and culture, like nowhere else."

—Hispanic friend

❖❖❖

"We don't know who we are; we don't think we deserve any more than we get; we expect to fail at everything regardless of all our efforts. That's the message we get from all sides, from schools and employers and people in authority. It breaks our spirits as we struggle to survive."

—A local Hispanic speaking about the damage done to a person by the pervasive 'cultural disparagement' over the years

❖❖❖

"Family is a simple word. But I wonder if you Anglos understand what it means to us Hispanics. For you it seems to refer to the small group of people who raised you, whom you can easily leave behind. But for us the word is rich with relationships A huge, warm multigenerational cluster of relatives, with complicated webs of tradition, associations and obligations. We cherish our day-to-day contacts and the love and support we give to each other. When family members leave the area, for schooling or jobs, it tears the fabric of family and causes pain that you Anglos apparently seldom feel. So when you casually use words like "education" or "success" or "professional advancement," which imply moving away from family, the words contain as much threat as promise."

—Hispanic social scientist

❖❖❖

"I grew up in a multicultural community surrounded by blondes, brunettes and black-haired people. I was one of the last, my hair as black as an Indian's. I always felt somehow inferior to the blondes who often called me names and were brutal to me, even though my family was mostly White. I deferred to those blondes, worshipped them, followed them, imitated them. They were the bright ones, the leaders, the ones who knew the answers and had influence everywhere. Not me. It took me years to get over this self-disparagement and claim my own place in the world."

—A Hispanic friend, now a community leader

❖❖❖

"Those women were formidable! The ones I was talking with yesterday. They are working full time to put food on the table. They are studying full time for professional degrees. They are tending their families: husbands, kids, households full time—and to their vast extended clans, too. They have time left over for involvement in their churches and community organizations, and for smiles and conversation with us visitors. Where do they get the energy?

"They are becoming teachers, lawyers, social workers. They are studying finance, communication, business. Their dedication and determination are impressive. They're resisting the pressures of cultural traditions (stereotype!) of homebound women. What a difference they and their predecessors are making, with their special Hispanic warmth pervading their skilled careers.

"But they are mostly invisible unless we're looking for them. How many of them are already practicing their professions in the outside world.? How many Indian women are out there doing the same thing? Why don't we see more of them? Why do we consider this unusual?

"This particular group was raising scholarship money to help other Hispanic women continue their education. They said that stereotypes and prejudice, within and beyond their communities, are still factors they deal with every day, but their very presence is making a difference—slowly.

"What may be 'normal' for Anglo women is not for our Hispanic and Indian friends. Let's work to help them make it so."

—An impressed *Vecinos* visitor

❖❖❖

"Families? People talk about the strength of Hispanic families. Don't I wish! Mine has so much pain, everybody hurting for one reason or another,

and I don't know why in most cases. People are always yelling at each other. Fighting, drunk, or on drugs; in and out of jail; no money, no jobs, no skills; babies coming along with no future . . . whadamess. No time, no caring, no place, no hope for ME. I got out as soon as I could."
—Homeless Hispanic

Anglos

Anglos are a diverse lot of people. Many have become a solid middle class, developing businesses and professions and participating in community life according to their interest and skills. Many others often try, as so many Anglos, to reshape the place they now live into the places they might have left behind. Many are well meaning in many ways, but sometimes unaware of intercultural dynamics that might surround them.

More Voices

"I was new to the area, pretty ignorant. I had a job and a mentor. I didn't realize he was Hispanic. He seemed like a good guy, and we worked well together. We laughed at and worried about the same sorts of things and played catch with green apples. I was hearing his name as a perfectly good American one with a slight local accent. Then one day I saw his name written. I was puzzled—who was this person? I watched and listened for a couple of days, seeking more signs, and finally accepted that my friend was really one of the Hispanics so maligned by my family and associates. I didn't say anything, but my mind had changed course, and our friendship deepened and expanded."
—An Anglo friend

❖ ❖ ❖

"Family? Mine are scattered all over the place. We hear from each other occasionally, but seldom meet in person. Our lives are all so different. We came here to get away from everything, to start fresh. We love it here: the scenery, the arts, the museums, the opera, the fiestas . . . we created our own 'new family,' by choice rather than biology, with the many friends we've made here."

—Retired Anglo

❖❖❖

"I'm not sure most people want to get deeply involved with people from another culture."

—Nervous Anglo

❖❖❖

"It's scary to be confronted with who you are in dialogue with people from other cultures. You feel totally vulnerable and afraid that maybe, in spite of your self-expectations, you are a racist after all."

—Another nervous Anglo

❖❖❖

"I'm a very curious Hispanic. I, and many others like me, want to know you, to know who you are. Please speak with us, invite us in for a cup of coffee, give us a chance to know you!"

—A "curious" Hispanic

❖❖❖

"I feel so bad about the fragility of the Hispanic and Indian cultures here, and wonder what caring Anglos can do to respect and strengthen them."

—A caring Anglo

❖❖❖

"I feel sorry about the tendency of caring Anglos to exploit and trivialize the local cultures while trying to 'save' them."

—A caring Hispanic

❖❖❖

"Most of us don't really know who we are, but through contacts with Indian and Hispanic friends I'm beginning to find my own roots, my traditional values, my strengths."

—Another Anglo

❖ *6* ❖

Stereotypes and Prejudices

*B*asically, they go together. The first, stereotypes, is based on expectations of how a person is or will behave, and could be either positive or negative. The second, prejudice, is a usually negative assumption, often inherited, of a person's worth or value.

Both keep us from seeing the real person. Both are over simplifications and usually false.

"Stereotypes make people invisible," insists Roberto Chene of the Southwest Center For Cross-Cultural Relationships. "People see only what they expect to see in the other person and ignore the diversity and the individuality of those in different ethnic and cultural groups."

❖❖❖

"Categories are extremely useful," says Laura Clarke, Anthropologist. "They summarize a general heritage, cultural experience, worldview. But they have to be used with sensitivity and caution because so many of us don't fit our expected cultural molds."

❖❖❖

Labels—ethnic, cultural or racial—can be sources of pain or of affirmation. How can we see them as useful handles and still perceive the varied individuals within the categories? How can we celebrate the strengths of our different heritages and help members identify with the positive elements of each? Bashing our own culture can lead to lopsided guilt trips. Bashing other cultures can also be unrealistically unfair. Every culture has positive and negative elements: how can we keep them in balance and avoid the easy stereotypes, particularly in times of conflict and tensions? This is one of the difficult problems of our time.

❖❖❖

One of the ways in which Roberto Chene helps people break down stereotypes is to set them in cross-cultural pairs and have each in turn just *listen* to the other talking about his or her life. Ten minutes seem like an interminable time to expose oneself to a stranger. One feels vulnerable, a bit silly, eager for forbidden feedback, uncertain of the other's reaction to your story. And it's a long time to listen without comment or interruption. But the experience really shifts perceptions, opens up a sharing between real and complex people, and puts human faces on the ethnic/cultural labels.

Perhaps we all need to listen to each other in this way.

Stereotypes:

Stereotypes are expectations of the actions, behavior and attitudes of people or groups other than our own.

They can be positive or negative, and they are everywhere. Stereotypes are easy, convenient, simplistic, unanalyzed. We accept them without thinking. They help us make "sense" out of our complex world, especially when our information is limited. We all use stereotypes occasionally, stereotyping others as we in turn are stereotyped.

Stereotypes can be used, abused, or both. They are influenced by our reading, heritage, politics, media, experiences, work, communities, friends and contacts. They are frequently manipulated by interest groups of all sorts. They affect our relationships and almost everything we do and stand for. They often ignore changing cultural realities, stuck in the past.

Stereotypes tend to "stuff" people and perspectives into "boxes" where they are perpetuated and solidified. There's nothing particularly "wrong" about stereotypes in general. They can paint a broad picture of conditions inviting further investigation. As they reflect a general background there may be some truth in them, but such "truth" is partial, incomplete, skewed, misleading.

We need to open the "boxes" and look at the creatures trapped inside:

To appreciate the diversity of people and perspectives released;
To free the insights they can offer for us all;
To help us improve our troubled and vibrant community.

You surely have been a victim of stereotyping at some time in your life. By whom? How? Why? How did it feel to be plopped down in a category that didn't represent you? How did you struggle against the confining "box" of other people's expectations? Or did you? What effect did such a "box" have on your relationships and ability to get things done? And on your own self-confidence? How could you clarify the "real you" and hold your head up high?

How can we crack open stereotypes?

We can meet stereotyped people as individuals.
We can listen to their stories, their joys and struggles and share our own.
We can look deeper into their backgrounds, their heritage, their history.
We can make multifaceted friends across the cultures.
We can work together on projects that concern us all.
We can relax and enjoy their company and their perspectives.
We can share food, fun, hospitality.
We can laugh together when ridiculous stereotypes get smashed.

And we may emerge with different stereotypes.

Prejudice:

Prejudice is an attitude that often evolves from stereotypes. It can be either positive or negative. Prejudice targets certain groups for exclusion or privilege regardless of merit. Codified by law or custom, outdated prejudice can last for generations. Prejudice, lodged deep in the psyche, is hard to eradicate even when external conditions change.

Prejudice affects all of life with the opportunities, challenges, restrictions and relationships available. Prejudice is a two-way street, affecting the perpetrators well as the targets. Prejudice justifies a need for political, social and economic dominance by one group over another. Prejudice perpetuates fear, favoritism, or fawning for survival.

Stereotypes represent an attitude, based on tradition rather than information. They can be mitigated with experience.

Prejudice, often based on stereotypes, leads to action, either active or passive, to control a population and its culture. Buried in a value system, it is very difficult to change.

Both affect individuals, lives and communities.

The Black Legend

It all started with the best of intentions.

When young Bartolome de las Casas arrived in Spain's Caribbean settlements in the early 1500s, he was appalled at the abuse of the Native Taino people. Many of the settlers and soldiers enslaved, tortured, raped, killed, massacred them, casually, at will, for fun, to the brink of extinction. A Dominican priest, and later a bishop, Las Casas dedicated his life to bring justice and humane treatment to the Native people of the New World.

He wrote scathing letters to the authorities in Spain describing what he was seeing with dramatic details, with the intention of shaming the Spanish government and bringing reform. Back and forth across the ocean he went, speaking, writing, raising allies until the outcry brought changes. The letters were printed, translated into various languages, and circulated widely within and beyond Spain itself. They were read and discussed everywhere.

Throughout this era Spain was at war, politically and religiously, with many of the northern European countries. For them these letters, illustrated with gory woodcuts, told the world what evil people the Spaniards were. It was marvelous propaganda to justify their enmity with the "cruel, brutal"

Spaniards, supported by the Pope and the nefarious Catholic Church. The propaganda was highly effective and produced a negative impression of everything Spanish that has lasted for generations. It is still embedded in unconscious prejudice, especially in Anglo/Protestant America, even here in New Mexico.

This prejudice is referred to as "The Black Legend."

But that's only part of the story.

In the early 1500s, there was considerable confusion about the Native people of the New World. Were they human? Were they sub-human savages fit only for exploitation and slavery? Could they be educated? Christianized? Did they have souls? Did God care about them? How should they be treated? This was a huge theological problem, debated again and again for many years.

Bartolome de las Casas believed strongly in their humanity, in their God-given souls, in their right to life and dignity. Over the years he interspersed his many trips to Spain, speaking and writing, initiating conferences and debates at the highest levels, with his work in America with Native people. There he developed new approaches to lead the Native people to Christ with kindness rather than the fear and force so pervasive at the time. As innovative Bishop of Oaxaca his influence increased, and he became known as The Apostle of the Indies.

The result? Over the years, various series of laws were promulgated, eventually codified in several volumes. They dealt with every phase of colonial life. Laws were strict regarding the Indians. They could not be enslaved. They had to be paid for their work, with ample time off for their own subsistence and ceremonies. They could be converted to Christianity by "gentle persuasion" but not by threats and force. They could be educated. Their elders and their traditions should be respected as much as possible. And so much more.

These Laws of the Indies were the most humane documents of any colonial power of the era. There was constant discussion, support and resistance to them over the years. Those who valued the Indians only for their labor, forcing them into slavery in the mines and fields and factories, resented any mitigation of their condition. Abuses continued, and the law courts were far away. For the "exploiters," their fortunes were more important than their expendable workers. For the "humanists," justice and fair treatment and the rule of law were more important. Many of the exploiters were brought into law courts for judgment and appropriate punishment, while others escaped through enormous bribes.

Yet the Laws of the Indies and the work of Fray Bartolome de las Casas express a vital part of the Spanish character and heritage, even here in New Mexico. Like two sides of a coin, it should be remembered, even though the Black Legend lives on.

What do you see in each of the following "*Vecinos* Vistas" in terms of Stereotypes and Prejudice?

Vista 1:

A little Indian girl ran up to an Anglo newcomer. "Hi," she greeted her with a big smile.

The Anglo had a sudden flashback to all the John Wayne movies she had grown up with. "Hi" wasn't the way Indians talked. Instinctively she raised her hand in a gesture of peace, and solemnly intoned, "How!"

The little girl giggled and ran off.

Later, the Anglo woman told the story on herself with a mixture of humor and embarrassment. "I wasn't making fun of her," she insisted. "I just didn't know any better."

How would you respond to this story? Why?

❖ ❖ ❖

Vista 2:

A potluck party involving some Tewa (Pueblo) and Anglo women. Good food, good conversation. I noticed two of the women, one Tewa and one Anglo, in intense conversation over cake and coffee.

Later, each of them spoke to me separately—the one from San Ildefonso, traditional and with only basic education, the other from the hills of Tennessee, with master's degree and flourishing counseling practice. Each commented that they had been sharing their parents' admonitions not to venture beyond their "own kinds of people," because "it's dangerous out there," and that they suddenly realized that they had many things in common.

What do you think is going on here, beyond mere words?

❖❖❖

Vista 3:

An Anglo grumbles, "I don't get it. These Hispanic folks are always complaining. We outsiders have taken away their land, their culture, their language. Yet everywhere I look, in city and state government, in local businesses, in the school system and other places, there are lots of their people in positions of power and influence. Why aren't they doing something creative about it if these conditions are so bad?"

What would you have said to this man?

❖❖❖

Vista 4:

I remember how upset I was when a Hispanic friend I'd been working with for some time said something seriously linking me with the Anglo consumer culture, never having noticed nor listened to my aversion to it. I jumped up and down and hollered that he was lumping me together with a kind of people I didn't relate to. He countered by jumping up and down and hollering that, just because he was Hispanic, I wanted him to act like my picture of how a Hispanic ought to act.

The laughter of some onlookers sobered us, and we started to laugh too, until our "hollering" turned into eye-tearing, gut-shaking belly laughs. It was an educational process for us both.

You probably would have laughed too. Why?

❖❖❖

Vista 5:

Santa Fe Trail Day on the Plaza. Scruffy-looking mountain men, traders, horses, pack mules, wagons, all milling around in splendid confusion. The New Mexico governor of 1821, represented by Tom Chavez, the then director of the History Museum, welcoming First Trader William Bucknell with hilarious repartee reflecting the Santa Fe of 1821 with the current 1996 ambience. Delighted bystanders, shivering in the icy wind, were almost all gray-haired Anglos.

I spotted a Sioux friend leaning against a tree, watching the scene. I went over to talk with him.

"I get a big kick out of this sort of event," he said. "Historical recreations like this bring the past alive for me, no matter how distorted. They make me think about things in new ways. But I feel guilty about being here at all. We all know what the coming of the White Man did to my people. Most of my friends would condemn me for being here and enjoying it. It's not 'politically correct,' but it's such fun!"

What would you say to my Sioux friend at this point?

❖ ❖ ❖

Vista 6:

A radio interviewer, obviously seeking 'points' with his Hispanic listeners, asked me when I was describing our aims with *Vecinos*, "Don't you just HATE all these rich Anglo newcomers who build their fancy houses on top of the mountains and try to make Santa Fe another Dallas or Los Angeles?"

What might you have responded?

❖ ❖ ❖

Vista 7:

All Species Day at Fort Marcy Park. People and their kids dressed as animals, from elk to butterflies to long-tailed tigers. Skits, music, storytellers, food, information booths. A skydiver landing amidst the festivities, a wonderful dance-drama with stilt-walking "cranes," a Noah's Ark story, and so much more. Fun and fascinating. Most participants were young Anglos, with kids and dogs in tow.

Leaving the park, I met a Hispanic friend, a well-traveled, sophisticated businessman.

"What's going on?" he inquired.

I described with considerable delight what was happening. "Go over and take a look. You'll enjoy it," I suggested.

"No, I don't think I will," he responded. "It looks like an Anglo thing. I don't expect I'd be welcome."

Do you think the man's fears were justified? What would you say to him?

❖❖❖

Vista 8:

An elderly Anglo friend who has lived in Santa Fe for a long time: "When I was growing up in New York City, the only Indians I knew about were those pesky redskins in Western movies riding horses, yipping fiercely, chasing cowboys and soldiers, slaughtering helpless settlers. I still have problems imagining Indians in any other way. Those movie Indians seem more real to me than 'real' Indians."

What childhood images still shape your ideas about Indians?

❖❖❖

Vista 9:

An Anglo man protests, vehemently. In a public meeting a Hispanic leader had referred to the Anglos as "obsessed with money and material things and with exploiting other people."

The Anglo had shouted, "We are not all like that! We have many different ideas and values, and some of them are closer to yours than you give us credit for. Lots of us are at war with the consumerism and exploitation we see around us and prove it with our lives if you care to look. Talk about stereotypes! You think we stereotype YOUR people, but you sure do it to ours too. It's not fair!"

How would you have responded to this situation?

❖❖❖

Vista 10:

Another Anglo: "An Indian is an Indian is an Indian. They've all got the same problems. Why can't they all work together to resolve them sensibly? I resent my money going to a bunch of government-supported deadbeats."

What does this guy have to learn?

❖❖❖

Vista 11:

An Anglo friend who delights in the cultural diversity of her acquaintances works in one of the state offices. "Some of my coworkers there shun me," she laments. "They refer to me as 'just another blue-eyes,' even though they can see that my eyes are brown, if they ever care to look. They reject me even before they know anything about me. It hurts!"

What do you think is going on here?

Stereotypes often persist in the back of our minds even when we "know better." For me, unexpected "Smashed Stereotypes" are delights. Some examples:

Stereotype: An Apache psychologist/medicine man in a very serious talk about his work.

Smashed: Returned after break with his Apache Country Western Band, with drums, guitars, accordion and more, sharing and teaching lively songs of his heritage with a joy that lasted for hours in my mind.

❖❖❖

Stereotype: Pueblo girls are docile and don't go far from their community.

Smashed: Handsome Pueblo woman who looks elegant in traditional garb and tells stories about her people and drives huge semi-trailer trucks cross country for a living.

❖❖❖

Stereotype: A Sioux family living in a tipi on the edge of town.

Smashed: Orders a huge pizza with all the fixings, to the astonishment of the delivery boy.

❖❖❖

Stereotype: A sophisticated businessman with cool sunglasses, stylish haircut, attaché case, long coat, shiny shoes.

Smashed: Uncovers to reveal Corn Dance regalia, with fox tail swinging from his kilt, rattles and green branches in his hands, jingling shells around his ankles, soft moccasins on his feet, as he steps out to join his Pueblo dancers on this feast day.

❖❖❖

Stereotype: A voluble Hispanic man talking with an Anglo.

Smashed: Who listens to people and doesn't get paid for it.

❖❖❖

Stereotype: The leader of a small, traditional pueblo.

Smashed: Who has graduate degrees from . . . Princeton!

❖❖❖

Stereotype: A well-known weaver from a small village who seldom leaves her farm.

Smashed: Who spends three months every year in Japan teaching her craft, and she sends ahead of her cases of the *chile* she can't live without.

❖❖❖

Stereotype: Sioux anger at Protestant missionaries as "culture destroyers" of their Indian culture.

Smashed: By one Sioux who upholds those missionaries as advocates and supporters of the people they serve.

❖❖❖

Stereotype: Pueblo women deeply involved with their traditional pueblo.

Smashed: Who have just returned from an international conference in . . . China!

And so on. What stereotype smashers have you encountered?

❖   *7*   ❖

Heritage

"*W*e ignore our heritage, the history and lifeways of our people, at our peril. Much of our heritage, what has gone before, the imbedded memories and values of parents, family and community, shape who and what we are and our attitudes toward each other and our world."

–Carol

Cultural Memories

*S*ome groups have long cultural memories. "The way it was," things that happened long ago, feuds and friendships from past generations are very much part of present realities.

Yet other groups, more recent immigrants whose families cast off their past to begin a new and better life in this New World, are focused on the present with very short memories. The former see themselves as stewards of a long and valued tradition. The latter see themselves as creators of a new and ever-hopeful future.

These viewpoints affect almost everything that is happening in our area. Land, water, development, education, jobs, justice, tourism, newcomers–the list of current and perpetual concerns is a long one. All are rooted deep in what has gone before. It is essential for us to consider the past as we move forward into the future.

Our heritage affects our values, which are hard to talk about until they are challenged. We cannot assume that we all agree on the things important to us. And heritage is hard to talk about when our schools and media consistently ignore the contributions of different cultural groups.

Yet these are areas essential to consider as we talk with our New Mexico neighbors, build relationships, and broaden our appreciation of the things for which people live and die.

New Mexico Timeline

1200s–1300s: Abandonment of Ancestral Pueblos (Anasazi) in the Four Corners region and the rise of the Rio Grande Pueblos.

1492–1542: Columbus reached the New World and Spaniards conquered, explored and settled much of the Americas.

1540–1542: Coronado's expedition reached New Mexico and beyond.

1598: Don Juan de Oñate began the first Spanish settlement in New Mexico, San Gabriel, near the confluence of the Chama and Rio Grande.

1609–1610: Don Pedro de Peralta founded Santa Fe under a royal charter.

1610–1680: Spanish settlements in Northern New Mexico. Franciscan Missions to convert, protect and Hispanicize the Native people. Expanded conflicts between mission and civil authorities festered. On the Camino Real from Mexico City periodic wagon trains brought supplies for the colonists. Spanish systems were often harsh, oppressive to the Indians.

1680: During the Pueblo Revolt, Pueblo people unified under Popé, killed many Spanish settlers and priests, drove the rest out of the area, and tried to destroy all vestiges of Spanish presence.

1692: The Spaniards returned under Governor Don Diego de Vargas.

1693–1821: During the Spanish Colonial period, Spanish/Pueblo relationships improved. Cultural blending led to "Indo/Hispanic" or "Hispano/Indian" heritage of today. Raids by hostile tribes—Comanches, Apaches, Navajos were a constant danger. Fears of French, English and American incursions into Spanish territory raised tensions. Spanish government controlled all trade. New Mexico was an isolated backwater with few resources.

1821: Mexico gained independence from Spain. Chaos reigned. Santa Fe Trail opened, bringing goods from the East and contacts with American traders.

1846–1847: U.S. War with Mexico. New Mexico was annexed as a U.S. Territory. The Treaty of Guadalupe-Hidalgo guaranteed traditional rights to Indian and Spanish people of the area.

1850: Bishop Lamy began the work of reforming the Catholic Church, bringing in social, medical and educational services, and "modernizing" New Mexico in many ways.

1862–1865: During the Civil War, a Confederate invasion was turned back at Glorieta Pass. In the Indian wars, Navajos and Apaches were rounded up and driven into exile at Bosque Redondo. U.S. military presence was essential.

1850–1900: American takeover brought in new laws, language, customs, perspectives. Treaties were ignored. Exploiters grabbed lands and resources. Railroad arrived in 1880. Anglo influence and Protestant missions conflicted with traditional perspectives.

1900–1941: The Selling of Santa Fe included artists, health sanatoria, Harvey Hotels, Santa Fe "Detours" for tourists, a resurgence of traditional crafts for the tourist trade, architectural styles that reflect historic heritage. New Mexico became a state in 1912. Depression, followed by government projects to develop parks, recreation areas, and arts/crafts.

1941–1945: World War II. New Mexican soldiers were captured by Japanese at Bataan. Wartime was marked by development of Los Alamos and the atom bomb, a detention camp for Japanese Americans, jobs for everyone, and an economic shift from barter to cash transactions.

1945–1980: These years saw tremendous growth and development of Santa Fe and New Mexico, gentrification of traditional neighborhoods, hippies and counter–culturalists, tourism, arts, "destination travel," cultural conflicts, ethnic tensions, Land Grant wars and more.

1980–2012: Continued growth and diversity expanded Santa Fe. A fine, exciting place to live, but New Mexico is at the bottom of lists of national social problems—poverty, poor education, abuse and violence, drug and alcohol use, incarceration, and so much more. And, to me, intercultural relations are a primary cause.

Indo-Hispanic New Mexican Heritage

The Pueblos:

Many historians consider the Pueblo Revolt of 1680 the most important event in all of New Mexico history. The Spanish Colonial Government had ruled the Pueblo world with iron fists, medieval institutions, harsh religious doctrines, abuse and exploitation.

At last the Pueblo people had had enough. United for the first time under the leadership of the charismatic Tewa medicine man Popé, they drove the Spaniards out of their land.

Twelve years later, the Spaniards returned led by Governor Don Diego de Vargas, and Spanish colonists resettled the area. But this time relationships with the Pueblo people were different. Many of the previous abuses were mitigated, and a system more of cooperation than of conflict evolved. The Indians needed Spanish tools, hardware, animals, fabrics, foods. The Spaniards needed Indian labor, knowledge of the land, survival skills. The alliances they forged helped create the Indo-Hispanic culture of New Mexico.

The Indians, now down to nineteen active pueblos, kept their languages, customs, religious traditions and governments, as mandated by the Laws of the Indies. They shared with their Hispanic neighbors the riches and risks of their farming/ranching economy and the hazards of drought, plagues, floods, storms and raids by hostile Indians. There was much intermarriage, resulting in masses of brown-skinned, bright-eyed sturdy New Mexicans as a result.

The Hispanics:

Many Hispanic families still trace their presence in New Mexico to the 1500s and 1600s. Some were "pure European" Spaniards, but most were mixtures of various European and Indian lineages.

Santa Fe was (and is) the principal town and seat of government. The

Viceroy in Mexico sent governors, some excellent and some ineffective or corrupt, to rule the area in the name of the Spanish king.

The colonists spread out, creating small towns, villages and ranches, often next to Pueblo communities.

The Missions were headquartered at Santo Domingo Pueblo, where the administration offices and "Father Custos" were in charge. The priests—and there were never enough of them—were assigned to the various Pueblos and worked to Christianize and Hispanicize the Indians under their influence.

The Camino Real, the long, difficult, dangerous road to Mexico City, periodically brought huge wagon trains of goods the settlers could not make for themselves: hardware, tools, fancy fabrics, ceramics, medicines, weapons, books, the latest fashions, religious and luxury items, wine and chocolate. And news. Picture the excitement when a wagon train approached. In return, the colonists sent sheep, tanned hides, buckskin, cotton and wool blankets, stockings, piñon nuts, and many other things they made or bartered from the Indians.

Mexico gained its independence from Spain in 1821. For New Mexico, the most conspicuous advantage was the opening of the Santa Fe Trail, previously prohibited by Spanish law that forbade trade with any countries other than Spain. The wagon trains brought in all sorts of goods from eastern factories, farms and fisheries, and other sources. Shoes, hats, many kinds of fabrics, tinned food, sawmills, window glass, printing presses, the latest fashions, tools, books, cooking pots, sewing machines, candies, lamps, sugar, oysters (!), and so much more. Merchants set up their stores in Santa Fe and in the larger towns, and sent vendors everywhere, profoundly changing the material life of the New Mexicans.

The chaotic post-independence government of Mexico lost the war with the United States, ceding the whole northern part of its territory to the victors in 1848. The *Americanos* who swarmed into the area over the following years brought new language, new laws, new customs, new government, new religions, new values, new energy—and racism. Though many good people brought useful things and ideas, the new territory also brought exploiters out to make their fortunes at the expense of the local people. Though the Treaty of Guadalupe Hidalgo at the end of the war had guaranteed protection for Indian and Hispanic lands, religions, customs, and traditions, consortiums of lawyers and business people, typified by the infamous "Santa Fe Ring," used every means, fair and foul, to grab prime lands and to turn the "little brown brothers" into "good Americans." These practices were devastating to the Native people, threatening their livelihoods, heritage and their very souls. Though the Indians were somewhat protected within their Pueblos, the Hispanics were not. The damage inflicted still lingers.

World War II brought many changes. Thousands of young men joined the military and for the first time got a look at the wider world. Those in the Coast Artillery, stationed in the Philippines, were captured by the Japanese, endured the Bataan Death March, suffered years of brutal imprisonment, and their survivors were specially honored on their return. Los Alamos, "The Secret City on the Hill," employed hundreds of locals in unskilled and menial jobs, as well as the super-scientists and helpers. The economy shifted from barter to cash, as regular wages brought stability and bank accounts to village people.

Meanwhile, the "Selling of Santa Fe" as a tourist destination escalated. Both Indians and Hispanics were seen as romantic, and sometimes tragic, characters. They were painted by members of the burgeoning artist colonies, upgraded their pottery, weaving and other crafts, endured visitors with their endless questions and cameras. They were interesting, dramatic, colorful—and vanishing, and drew in visitors by the thousands.

The artistic skills of many are indisputable. The Indian and Spanish markets now bring in thousands of visitors and dollars each year. But that's not all. Indians and Hispanics can be seen in many occupations all over Santa Fe and New Mexico. They work in offices, businesses, technical jobs, education, community services, heavy labor. Many own their own establishments. Some go elsewhere for education and careers, and some of these return to offer their skills and experience to their home communities. But many others are locked away in depression and despair, unable to surmount the cultural barriers.

Now, the modern Anglo culture continues to roll over the Native populations without knowing how to communicate, listen, respect or understand the Indo-Hispanic heritage of their neighbors.

Mexican and New Mexican Hispanics seldom seem to get along. They are very different.

The recent Mexicans have come here fleeing poverty and violence, often at great risk to themselves. As with most immigrants everywhere, they arrive with a certain optimism and "git up and git." They work hard, raise families, start businesses, become citizens, follow the "American Dream." They speak good Spanish and swagger when they walk. They send money back to Mexico and send their kids to school. These kids become their interpreters (many parents don't speak much English) of American life and language. Those without official documents live in perpetual tension, anticipating raids by the "migra" that will break up their families with deportations. Cruel stories abound.

New Mexican Hispanics, on the other hand, have experienced generations of racism and cultural disparagement. In general, they lack the confidence and optimism of the Mexicans; their Spanish is an antique dialect from the sixteenth Century mixed in with Pueblo and English that we commonly call "Spanglish." "We speak the language of Cervantes," old folks sometimes say with pride—but that's only partly true. Memories go back generations to the loss of land and culture, and the massive efforts of the media and educational systems to eradicate their heritage. The interests of the young people are alienating, for they generally have little knowledge or understanding of their own heritage. Many Hispanics are struggling to hold onto their culture and values, others have already abandoned them. But it's not easy.

It's easy for New Mexican Hispanics to feel threatened by the Mexicans as they flow into the area, finding jobs, setting up homes and businesses. And it's easy for the Mexicans to disparage the local Hispanics as "passive, ignorant 'hicks.'" Just don't try to include them all under one umbrella. It doesn't work.

Observation by a Mexican resident:

"I don't sense much joy in the local Hispanics. I miss the spontaneous singing, exuberant dancing, laughter, joking, fun, witticisms, and a certain creativity of mind. These are part of Mexican life even when times are tough. The local Mexicanismos all seem imported, from mariachis to folk dances. Is it because life was so hard here in the early days that all the joy was squeezed out of them? Or under American control they felt oppressed too hard? Or is it the struggle to keep some of their heritage intact under the pressures of the modern 'mainstream'? Quien sabe?"

8

Memorable Moments

Here are samplings of some events that have marked New Mexico's intercultural heritage in the past. Some came out happily. Some are still pending. Some illustrate warnings of dangers we face.

Samplings from the past, yes. But the present is full of events, moments and ongoing situations that affect the cultures of our region. Notice, observe, be aware of what's going on, for better or for worse.

Land Grants—Do They Still Matter?

Mention Land Grants to an Anglo and you'll probably receive a look of puzzled indifference. To a Northern New Mexican Hispanic a series of intense expressions may flit across his (or her) face. Though they date from long ago, their impact is still vital.

Under the Spanish Colonial land system, huge tracts of land were awarded in the name of the king to prominent individuals and to communities, their families and their heirs. The Treaty of Guadalupe-Hidalgo in 1848, when the Americans annexed New Mexico, guaranteed rights to these lands to the heirs of the original grantees. For the Indian and Hispanic people, the system worked as a source of their rootedness and value. It provided places they called home, identification, relationships with their neighbors, and a promise for the livelihood of future generations. Land meant life, and it was their precious heritage.

When the American government came in during the 1850s, land issues were the most difficult things they had to deal with. The Americans had no such emotional attachment to the land: it was simply a commodity to use, to buy, to sell, on which to produce profits. American and Spanish Colonial Laws were in direct conflict, legally, commercially, and philosophically. Land was a prime resource, and many Anglo "land barons" wanted to acquire it, by fair means or foul. And besides, the Hispanics who lived on the lands seemed like "simple people" to the Anglos, easy to dupe, of no particular account.

Stories still linger of the many ways in which land-grabbers like those in the Santa Fe Ring operated. Here are some of them:

When the American administrators moved into the Palace of the Governors, they threw out stacks of "waste papers" to be burned. Later they realized that these were the original deeds to the land grants all over the state. Without them nobody could "prove" ownership except by "tradition," which American law did not recognize.

Anglo surveyors were sent out to measure the land "properly," because American law did not recognize the "natural" markers that were commonly used—trees, rocks, streams. It was easy for them to add a bit here, change a bit there, and refute any protests with blizzards of English, which the locals did not understand.

Spanish law did not tax land. Anglo law did. This was something totally new for the local Hispanics, and it seemed somehow immoral. In accordance with American law, notices appeared in English language newspapers that back taxes were due on a certain tract of land, and if they were not paid by a certain date the land would be confiscated. Hispanics never saw the notices nor knew what was happening. Imagine surprised landowners waking up one morning to find police or soldiers on their doorsteps with news that their land was no longer theirs and that they had to get out immediately. No warning, no recourse, no law-savvy allies. Not yet were there any of the sharp bilingual, bicultural Hispanic lawyers available now to come to their rescue.

Spanish law allocated to each settler enough land for house, garden and domestic use, and to the communities large tracts of common land for grazing livestock, woodcutting, hunting and foraging. American law did not recognize this common land and confiscated it. Much of it ended up in the U.S. Forest Service, *la floresta* to the locals, which increasingly tried to limit the villagers' access to it. Environmental protection versus traditional grazing rights have come into conflict every year. A lot of anger and threats of violence simmered beneath the surface.

Most of these things happened long ago. Why do they still fester? You may well ask.

Because they are part of a pattern that continues, in subtle ways, to eradicate the old traditions in order to "Americanize" everybody. And because they are happening still.

"Your house is on my land," a Hispanic person may say to you (presumably you are an Anglo). "This land belongs to my family. Your people stole it from us and paid us nothing. If they had bought it legally and paid a fair price, we would be rich, or at least have enough money for our needs. Which we don't." *(I have seen this happen several times.)*

A developer advertises his new project as "built on such-and-such land grant," which sounds to outsiders ancient and romantic. But the land grant heirs look at it differently. They see land, which used to be theirs, making money of which they should be getting a share.

Occasionally, the heirs of a land grant get together to hire smart lawyers to sue present landowners for some sort of recompense. The cases drag on for years in the hopes that people will die off or give up. Yet sometimes the heirs win!

Water rights traditionally go with the land and are carefully parceled out to the people who live and farm there. Developers buy out these rights from old folks who die or move off the land, weakening the whole structure of the communities. Water Law is a complex business, constantly being adjudicated in the courts.

Many books document land grabs and some of the nefarious schemes by which local people have been defrauded of their heritage. If you think these are only things of the past, read the papers, listen to people, ask questions.

The Bursum Bill—1922

This is one of my favorite stories of intercultural cooperation.

Throughout the 1910s, the official status of the Pueblo Indians was in great confusion. The Pueblos were actually poor, struggling for survival and dignity. The United States government, in its great wisdom, decided that the Pueblos were sufficiently "civilized" to manage their own affairs without protective government oversight. Ten years later, the government changed its mind.

The Pueblos were desperately poor and about their only resource was their land, of which they had plenty. Though the Treaty of Guadalupe Hidalgo protected ownership of the land, during these years much of the land was sold, rented, or settled by squatters the Indians could not dislodge. Grabbing Indian land was a regular road to riches for settlers. Some say as many as five thousand non-Indians were living on Indian land by 1920.

Holm O. Bursum, a senator from New Mexico, attached a rider onto a larger bill going through Congress. This "Bursum Bill" said that all the non-Indians settled on Indian land would become official owners on a certain date. The bill was hidden away amidst other legislation in the hopes that nobody would notice, or care.

That almost happened.

Young John Collier was staying with friends in Taos when someone from the East sent him a copy of this Bursum Bill. He took copies of it to the headmen of all the local pueblos. They were appalled. They had received no information about any such legislation, even though it would affect them directly. The loss of so much of their land would ruin their people for generations, destroy their livelihoods and cultures, and force them into complete destitution. So they feared. What could they do?

John Collier came to their rescue. He gathered all the Pueblo leaders together, persuaded them to form the All Indian Pueblo Council—the first unification since the Pueblo Revolt in 1680, and to send a delegation to Washington to fight for their land, which the Treaty of Guadalupe Hidalgo had guaranteed to them. Then he mobilized all his friends among the artist communities, who were much concerned about the Indian subjects of so many of their paintings. They contacted families, friends, relatives, politicians, business people, financiers—people of influence all over the country. The national chain of women's clubs, which were influential at that time, took up the cause. Intense discussion and outrage sent a powerful message to Washington.

And the Bursum Bill was defeated! The non-Indians had to return or pay rent on the occupied land to the Pueblos. The Pueblo people and the Treaty of Guadalupe Hidalgo had won the day.

John Collier later became a highly effective U.S. Commissioner of Indian Affairs.

The Tierra Amarilla Courthouse Raid—1967

It was the 1960s, years of Civil Rights ferment all over the country. Oppressed people were raising their voices everywhere—except here.

Northern New Mexico was (and still is) dotted with traditional Hispanic villages, the residents struggling for survival, cherishing their traditional ways of life. Farming. Woodcutting. Raising livestock. Mostly, they were peaceful people, unwilling to cause problems, but with an undercurrent of anger that could explode into violence when provoked.

Along came Reies Tijerina. Mexican born, he had been a Pentecostal preacher in the Texas Border country. He was appalled at the passivity of the local Hispanics and urged them to fight for their rights and their dignity. Many people listened.

Under his influence, he and the people formed *La Alianza* (The Alliance); they proclaimed themselves The Republic of San Juan and officially seceded from the United States. They wanted to call attention to the many injustices their people had suffered, to reclaim use of the land grants denied them by the government, to acquire enough power to negotiate for their needs. They needed to be noticed.

They burned signs of the hated *floresta*. They kidnapped forest rangers.

The held protest marches and rallies. They cut fences, burned barns, seized land. Pickup trucks bristling with gun toting villagers carried their "authority" throughout the region. They stopped cars, issued passports, and claimed locations as far away as Albuquerque. Over the months, their presence surely WAS felt, though it wasn't taken too seriously.

But then came the raid on the old yellow courthouse in Tierra Amarilla. The raid was in retaliation for the arrest of some of their members at a land grant protest. In the mêlée, shots were fired and a couple of people were wounded. (Picnickers, including a friend of mine, watched in disbelief from a nearby hillside.) At the sight of blood, the locals panicked and fled into the mountains.

The Lieutenant Governor, who was in charge that day, also panicked. He couldn't permit an armed rebellion to escalate. He called out the National Guard, with soldiers, a helicopter, and tanks! The tanks could not maneuver on the rough mountain trails, the helicopter could not see through the foliage, the foot soldiers found Anglo fishermen but no fugitives. Besides, many of the pursuers were sympathetic to the *Alianza* goals, and didn't want to apprehend their compatriots.

Eventually, Reies Tijerina was captured. He defended himself at his trial and was acquitted, to the delight of Hispanics and oppressed people everywhere. Later, he spent time in prison on another charge and retired to a Northern New Mexico village. But without his charismatic leadership, *La Alianza* and the Republic of San Juan faded away.

The Anglo newspapers had had a field day. They portrayed the whole affair as a comic opera at its best. But the humor disguised the very real underlying tragedy: the sense of loss of their ancestral lands and the impoverishment of the traditional heritage of the New Mexican Hispanic people.

Blue Lake—1970

Blue Lake is sacred to the people of Taos Pueblo. According to tradition this is the "place of emergence," where their distant ancestors had risen from the underworld into this one. It has always been a place of pilgrimage and prayer, of ceremonies and memories. The lake sits among the mountains above the Pueblo, and is the source of the river that flows through the community, bringing life to the Pueblo and its people.

In 1906, the United States Government, by decree, annexed much of the mountain terrain, eventually awarding it to the Forest Service. Indian protests were ignored. The lake and much of the surrounding land were off-limits to the Taos people. The Forest Service encouraged commercial ventures on the land—logging, hunting, public recreation, and other profitable endeavors.

Strangers were desecrating the sacred space, and there wasn't much the Indians could do about it. For years they tried. They contacted all sorts of influential people asking for return of their sacred lands. Nobody paid attention, and their efforts were in vain.

But in the 1960s, people started to listen. It was the Civil Rights era, and calls for justice by minority people were heard all across the country. The Taos Indians redoubled their efforts, created public relations campaigns, contacted people of influence—and congressmen—all over the country. At last, their voices were heard. And in 1970, signed by President Nixon himself, a bill passed by Congress restored the Blue Lake and surrounding territory to the Taos Pueblo people. Rejoicing reverberated throughout the land.

Once again, Blue Lake and vicinity are dedicated to pilgrimage and prayer, of ceremonies and memories. It's a beautiful spot, sacred to the Taos Pueblo people.

NAGPRA
Pecos—1999

For four hundred years, Pecos, the easternmost of the Rio Grande Pueblos, had played an influential role in the history of New Mexico. Though the Pueblo was abandoned in 1838, its descendants, now affiliated with the Jemez Pueblo, have flourished.

In the 1910s and '20s, archaeologists excavated part of the Pueblo ruins, sending some two thousand human remains to Harvard University for examination and storage. It was a huge contribution and provided important information about the lives, land, and times of the Pecos Pueblo people over the generations. Among the grave goods included with the remains were many objects considered sacred.

In 1990, after years of dedicated work by countless advocates, mostly Indian, Congress passed the Native American Graves Protection and Repatriation Act, called NAGPRA. It mandated that universities and museums that received federal funds must return to appropriate tribes any human remains and sacred objects requested. The Pecos people were at the forefront of this movement, though the National Park Service now cares for their ancestral home.

Almost ten years were necessary for all the negotiations to be completed. It was a process complicated in many unexpected ways: chaotic collections that needed to be sorted out and computerized, a new Pecos Pueblo government with different perspectives every year, Harvard's reluctance to relinquish the skeletons, disagreements about disposal of the remains. Eventually, everything was in place.

May 22, 1999.

The first and the biggest repatriation of ancestral remains took place at the Pecos National Historical Park. It was estimated that fifteen hundred Indians in their finest, most colorful clothing were present for the burial, for the speakers and for the feasting. It was a great day, full of significance for Indians everywhere. The ancestors who had been stolen away had been returned to their homeland. The emotional impact of the event for Indian people cannot be overestimated. Justice had been served.

It didn't just happen. It was the result of years of dedicated work by Indian and Anglo people, tribes and institutions, individuals and committees, all working together. Incidentally, I was there and knew many of the people involved.

Would-Be Developers

Tierra Amarilla:

In the 1990s, developers eyed Tierra Amarilla. An Arizona company started buying tracts of land in this beautiful Northern New Mexico valley. Two thousand homes were planned, and the charts and spiels of their spokespeople were overwhelming. Yes, they would enrich the people of the valley and provide jobs, lots of jobs. There would be a shopping center with all sorts of fine goods from all over the world for sale. Rich people would bring culture and arts and sophistication to the area. It would be a destination to make people proud,

But what kind of jobs they didn't say. What effect would it have on the traditional life of the valley? Where would enough water come from for all these people? The Arizonians were convincing; they had plenty of money, statistics, personnel and persuasive skills. The local people were uncomfortable with the promises but didn't know how to fight.

One of the leaders stepped up. He recognized the dangers and had a plan. Under his direction, people dug a military-style bunker along the road into town. They staffed it night and day with citizens toting rifles and shotguns. They threatened to shoot any developers on sight. They invited newspaper reporters, politicians, social service workers, tour groups, government officials, passersby, all comers, to stop and hear their story. The Davids fighting the Goliaths to preserve their cherished New Mexican heritage. They offered coffee, informational flyers, and posters of a dramatic Zapata-like figure shouting "*Tierra o Muerte.*" Spokespeople were often there, hosting the visitors, making sure that they understood the situation. News spread all over the area, and Eastern newspapers picked up the story.

The standoff lasted several months. Eventually, the developers went away. "It's evident the people don't want us there," they lamented. "We could have made such a difference for those poor peasants. But we can't fight their hostility."

❖❖❖

Pecos:

The Greer Garson ranch (yes, that's the British movie actress) encompassed a large part of the Pecos Valley about twenty miles east of Santa Fe. Nearby were the village of Pecos proper and the National Historic Park protecting the ruins of the ancient Pueblo and the mission church that had served the Pueblo. Many homes, farms and guest ranches had spread throughout the area and up into the nearby canyon. But Greer was in a hospital, slowly dying, and needed to sell her beloved ranch.

Among the potential buyers, one stood out. He insisted he only wanted to build his own ranch house, care for the land and protect the environment. He had lots of money and could easily afford the price. Negotiations proceeded and were almost completed.

And then an enterprising reporter investigated. What he found was alarming. This man, this potential buyer, was a sleazy developer, under indictment for crooked deals back East. In spite of his promise to Greer, his plans were extensive. He intended to build a satellite city, a suburb to Santa Fe with a population of twenty thousand, and attractions that would draw in visitors from miles around. He planned a stock car racetrack, a state-of-the-art amusement park, a helicopter pad so close to the ruined church that the vibrations would topple the walls, a gambling casino, and much more.

Of course, the deal was off and the man went away in disgrace. But this possibility had come too close for comfort. Other arrangements were quickly made to protect the land and the life of the people of the valley.

❖ ❖ ❖

These are just two examples of attempted land-grabs I personally observed. But many more are happening all the time.

Did you see Robert Redford's movie, "The Milagro Beanfield War," or read the book of the same name by John Nichols? It's a light-hearted story of village people fending off evil developers. It's fiction, but its basic story is repeated frequently and calls us to watch what is happening.

Moments In Now

Watch the papers. Listen to the locals. Observe what's happening. You'll see that there's a lot going on regarding our intersecting cultures—if you care to notice. Each of the listed themes here has many subsets, some of which have been described in detail (2013).
Look at:

Land Issues. Use and abuse. Ownership. Land Grants. Who's in control? Who wants it? Law and the Courts.

Water Resources. Distribution. Who gets it? When? Why? In times of drought?

Development. Scarce resources. Ancestral claims. Rights and customs. Money talks—or does it?

Boundaries. Authority. Jurisdictions. Control.

Law/Justice. There's much tension here. More information, both positive and negative, would be useful.

Abuse. Substance and personal. Affects all communities, particularly Hispanic and Indian. Who is doing what to control it, with or without success?

Education. What works in our multicultural schools and what doesn't? Why? How can it be improved?

Economics. Projects that sustain cultural values, environment, technologies and training for the future. Intercultural cooperation and involvement.

Ceremonies. Reflect cultures, reassert values, strengthen the present and build for future generations.

Intercultural Relationships. Conflicts. Cooperation. Interactions. Resources for creative connections.

Many stories of each of these themes, and more, have attracted notice over the past few months. Sometimes they point to ways in which we, of whatever background, can help make a difference—for better or otherwise.

9

Cultural Values

Our Values

They Affect Our Attitudes About Almost Everything Happening Around Us.

They Determine What Is Important To Us And Why.

They Are Hard To Talk About Because We Seldom Think About Them Until They Are Challenged.

They Are Embedded In Our Subconscious Where We Don't Realize Their Effect.

They Are The Positive Motivators Of Whatever We Do, Say And Represent.

When Values Conflict, It Is Essential To Take Them Out And Look At Them.

Values May Conflict More In Style Than Substance, Or Not.

Who Are You? Where Do You Come From? What Do You Stand For? Why Are You Here?

Sometimes, for some of us, these questions are easy. Sometimes they are not. Sometimes they rear up and bite us, calling for attention, needing to be reconsidered.

"If you don't know who you are and what you stand for, you don't have much to offer." So say the pundits.

Most of us are works in progress. We're constantly learning and growing, becoming something more than what we were. None of us is simple. We're made up of multiple strands of influence, many of which shift over time with our age and experience.

One of the hardest things of all is to look critically at our long-embedded values, to see which ones are still relevant and which should be adapted or discarded. Unexpected events, alternative opinions, new contacts, changing contexts can all challenge our beloved beliefs, causing dismay and confusion in response.

We want to be able to express our beliefs clearly and confidently. Our values are important to us: they make us who we are. We want to share them, or use them to influence others. But when they are vague and mushy, they don't mean much.

It's comfortable when we're surrounded with people who share our basic values, our treasured beliefs. We don't have to think about them very much, we can relax amidst assumed harmony. It's scary leaving our comfort zone where unknown challenges can test everything we think and do. Yet, these very challenges can toughen us, they can open new doorways, they can reawaken forgotten viewpoints, they can stimulate passive minds, they can help us consider what we deem important. Scary, yes, but rewarding.

I think there are two kinds of values to consider. CORE VALUES are the bedrock, non-negotiable base at the center, the heart of our perceptions. PERIPHERAL VALUES cluster around the core, more flexible, varied, and open to change. The problem often is deciding which is core and which peripheral.

For instance, a core value might honor the dignity of all people, which ties together everything else. Clustering peripherals might include all sorts of things enhancing or relating to the dignity of people. For some of these peripherals, we will fight bloody battles for years, without recognizing their flexibility in relation to the underlying core. What is most important: the relevance of our history for today, or the way it is taught? The dignity of work, or the many definitions of what work can be? Loving domestic partnerships, or restrictions on which partnerships are valid?

How do we express these values? Mostly by the way we live our lives and what we do and say. Sometimes our values are inherited, unthinkingly absorbed from the context around us. Sometimes they result from long, conscious struggle considering the implications and responsibilities involved.

Sometime they are so flexible that we don't really know where we stand. And sometimes all of the above, depending on which of our many values is under consideration at the time.

When our values are challenged, we often become upset, defensive and resistant. Or we get angry, lashing out in inappropriate ways. Or we retreat into stony silence, licking our emotional wounds. Or maybe, just maybe, we stop to consider what has been said and what, if any, relevance it holds for us at this moment.

Sometimes we have to stand our ground as we recognize that our values are important and to express them in a way that convinces others as well as ourselves. And sometimes we realize that our (peripheral) values need to evolve to cope with changing perspectives and realities.

But most of all, we can welcome the situations that challenge our values, encouraging us to take them out to look at, to strengthen them, to deepen them, or adapt them to changing situations and perceptions. Then we really have something solid to offer.

Contrasting Cultural Values:

These have been a recurring theme in many of our *Vecinos conversaciónes.* At one of them, a psychologist and a social scientist, both Hispanic, set out for us some of the areas where traditional Hispanic and Anglo values are in direct conflict. To summarize:

Family

For Hispanics: Huge, extended, multigenerational, ongoing, connected. Primary source of mutual support, personal relationships, community action. A warm, nurturing nest where traditions are upheld, accomplishments celebrated, and family stories retold. Physically close, in the same household or community.

For Anglos: Usually a nuclear entity of parents and children, a launching pad for the young who may or may not continue close family relationships once grown and gone. Often spread out geographically. Family reunions with relatives often sources of stress: magazines provide articles about "surviving" such reunions.

Community

For Hispanics: Embedded in community. Webs of responsibilities to families, churches, organizations, and people. Decisions and actions by group: too much individual initiative distrusted, discouraged.

For Anglos: Anglos move around a lot. Many people are "free individuals" floating around among shifting groups, jobs, alliances, areas, relationships with transitory commitments to places and people. Individual initiatives and successes respected.

Faith

For Hispanics: Traditionally Catholic. Rich, ancient liturgies, much beauty and symbolism, God and the saints (and the priest and the Pope) in control. Room for deep-level mysticism and sense of the miraculous. Much outreach and care for the needy.

For Anglos: Many religious varieties, often Bible based, ranging from highly liturgical worship to folk-rock/gospel music, to silent waiting for the Spirit. Many degrees of formality, message, outreach, caring, community, and acceptance. Anglos 'follow the spirit' from church to church—or none.

Language

For Hispanics: The Spanish language holds together the core of Hispanic culture. It is charged with deep meanings, a source of connectedness among people and generations. In Northern New Mexico, *Spanglish* is the common mixture of antique Spanish, Pueblo languages and English, in a very special dialect developed over the centuries. Mexican Spanish does not have these linguistic intrusions, which makes communication often difficult.

Anglos happily discard their languages of foreign origin in favor of "English Only," melting happily in the pot with little knowledge of other languages and little respect for non-mainstream cultures and the people who speak those languages.

Tradition

Hispanics are generally oriented toward the past, remembering the "old days," caring for the "old ones," cherishing the wisdom of the ancestors. History, the Past, is still a vital part of "today."

Anglos are generally oriented toward the future, trying to improve on an imperfect past. Innovation, experimentation and risk taking are valued. History is a subject of study and romance, but not an integral part of present life.

Land

For Hispanics: People belong to the land. It's their heritage, their identity, a sacred trust for the next generations, to be cared for and fought for when necessary.

For Anglos: The land belongs to people, can be traded, sold, developed, discarded, abandoned. Little sentiment, it's an economic resource.

Time Sense

Hispanics traditionally look at the long view, see the present as connecting the past with the future in a long continuity. Planning is for the next "seven generations." Also, clock time is an Anglo-created convenience, with which Hispanics often have a relaxed relationship.

Anglos generally want quick results, for the immediate present. They seldom look far into the past or the future. And clock time is vital to keep track of their busy lives.

Education

Hispanics often resist formal schooling because so often it denigrates their culture and so much they hold dear. As it creates careers, it ruptures relationships with traditional cultures and draws young people away from their communities and families.

For Anglos: Education is essential for understanding and relating to the contemporary world and for finding their place in it. It opens opportunities for "getting ahead."

Success

For Hispanics: The focus is generally on family and relationships, on church, and care for the heritage and community. Material goods and money of less importance.

For Anglos: The focus is on accomplishments, on careers, on recognition by peers, on accumulating money and material possessions.

Look at the obituaries in newspapers. Many Hispanic accounts list family members across the generations and very little about what the person actually did. Anglos, however, list careers, work accomplishments, honors, with very little about family.

During the *conversaciónes,* both speakers lamented the loss of so many of the old Hispanic values and told vivid stories demonstrating the crumbling of the traditional culture. And both insisted that this cultural loss was essential, that to "make it" in the Anglo world, Hispanics had to discard the old thinking and adopt Anglo ways. "The prisons are full of Hispanic guys who couldn't adjust to the Anglo world," was one example cited. "Funerals are where Hispanics meet these days," lamented the other.

Lively discussion ensued. Which values do you think could be carried out into the Anglo world? Which ones do you think would benefit the Anglos? What does the Hispanic tradition have to offer the larger community? Clearly, the audience, mostly Anglos with a sprinkling of Hispanics and Indians, was much troubled by this lack of any affirmation of their own heritage by these two men.

As our *Vecinos* experience shows, assimilation of the cultures is much more complicated than merely "abandoning" the old Hispanic traditions.

❖❖❖

I remembered this *conversación* a couple of Saturdays later that I spent helping a group of people replaster an old chapel. What struck me was that these traditional Hispanic values that are "doomed to disappear" were so positively expressed in this setting.

Most of the workers belonged to one extended family, three generations of brothers, sisters, cousins, in-laws, aunts, a grandmother, young children, even a family dog. They had come from many miles around, giving up their Saturdays for the summer ahead to work together on this project. I could feel the close and caring ties among them, yet they made room for us outsiders among them.

Many of these people were "making it" in the Anglo world, yet without losing their Hispanic identity. They included a physician, a mechanical engineer, a nurse, a social worker, a bus driver, mothers of young children, among others, and they seemed very comfortable with who they were. They spoke Spanish *(Spanglish)* as much as English, sprinkling conversations with old sayings *(dichos)* and "words that enrich and bind," most of which, fortunately, I could understand.

Their "past orientation" seemed a source of great strength. They told us in rich detail about their ancestors who had settled the area and showed us where houses used to stand and about the individuals buried in the small graveyard. One was preparing a genealogy chart to help trace all relationships. They were relearning from their grandmother the skills of working with adobe and teaching us, as well as their own young folks. There was a sense of healthy continuity with the past, giving present people roots and an awareness of where they belonged. It was a good feeling for an Anglo a long way from home.

The chapel had been built by their forbears, but had been abandoned for fifty years and needed lots of repair. It was still the focus for their deep faith, and a tangible symbol of it, that was bringing them together. It had once been a beautiful little building, as it could be again.

They worked so well together as a group that I couldn't pick out any one person theoretically in charge. Hierarchical Anglo me kept looking for the "boss" to tell me what to do, to give directions, but it didn't work that way. Everybody helped, everybody was helpful, everybody seemed to know just what to do.

They were still talking about what had happened the week before. They had seen people approaching across the fields. It was a procession of Indians from the nearby Pueblo of Santa Clara. They had seen the activity at the old chapel, and were bringing back for a visit the statues of saints entrusted to them for safekeeping when the chapel was abandoned. They carried them inside the ruined building. Everybody joined for an impromptu ceremony of joy and thanksgiving and shared the food that all had brought. It was a time of tears and laughter, a very moving story as they told it.

As we helped them mix the mud and slather it on the walls, balancing on rickety scaffolding and hauling heavy buckets, we talked and shared stories. They fed us, and they made us feel welcome and told us that, in our own small way, we were contributing to the land and the people of our adopted home.

I felt deeply enriched by this contact with these old Hispanic values, as I interpreted them, which seemed so vibrantly alive among the people we met that day.

People Of Faith

Too bad that our religions so often separate us, we people of Northern New Mexico. On the other hand, the fact that most of us are "people of faith" could pull us together in many rich ways.

A friend commented recently that he couldn't visit the Santuario at Chimayó because he was so angry at the role of the conservative Catholic Church in Latin America. Another expressed irritation at the Fundamentalists' narrow interpretation of the scriptures and their arrogant self-righteousness. Another was too upset over the Israeli treatment of the Palestinians to consider becoming friendly with local Jews. Another loudly condemned "Mainstream Protestants" who are so liberal that "their brains fall out" . . .

Strange church buildings are intimidating: we often hesitate to go inside. Unfamiliar rituals tend to make us uncomfortable, whether High Episcopalian liturgy or the Quaker silence or Muslim prostrations toward Mecca. Historical memories of persecutors and victims in the name of religions often get in the way: Puritans burned witches, Catholics burned heretics. "Unrealistic expectations" of human perfectibility or sinfulness trouble our consciences. Resulting lifestyles, whether conspicuous turbans or frequent communions or devotion to painted and plaster *santos* seem strange and forbidding. Church hierarchies, bishops and councils and administrative bodies, making sweeping pronouncements often cause us to lose sight of the real people of religious faith around us.

Santa Fe is rich with many religious groups. Efforts of organizations like the Inter-Faith Council bring together some groups for service projects and celebrations. Otherwise, there is little relationship among them. For most of us, it is hard to talk about religion in a secular world when we are uncertain of our reception among our listeners, and we are often unsure of our own understanding of the religious body to which we are committed.

But faith pulls us together. Faith expresses a universal (almost) human need. We need a sense of connectedness: to the powers of the universe, to the transcendent God, to the Spirit that animates our lives, to guidance about our actions. There are spiritual presences within and around us, which connect us to the past, the future, and the worldwide present.

Faith takes on many expressions, according to our particular culture, era and experience. It provides values and continuity; it creates meaning and purpose for our lives; it strengthens and shapes our energies amidst the uncertainties of our changing times. Faith, in its many diverse manifestations, whether in the summer corn dances, or the Easter trumpets, or the solemn rituals of Yom Kippur, must be acknowledged, affirmed, and respected as a common yearning of the human experience.

Faith reflects *people* rather than religious "bodies," and it often escapes from formal religious boundaries. As we try to understand and to relate more effectively to our *Vecinos* in Northern New Mexico, let's think together about faith rather than religions, though the latter often shapes and expresses the former. Let's *see* the faith that sends pilgrims walking to Chimayó, the faith that brings scattered Pueblo people home for the dance cycles, the faith that sends volunteers out to the penitentiary and to nursing homes to remind lonely people that they are cared about, the faith that animates and enriches so many lives. No matter whether the *Vecinos* are Jewish or Pentecostal, Lutheran or Sikh, Catholic or Quaker, New Age or Orthodox, our faith, given an atmosphere of respect and caring, is something we can talk about, share, and demonstrate. From other People of Faith we can all learn and enrich our own perspectives in many ways. Even though we may have had different experiences, and may not agree with the conclusions of other people, the ongoing dialogues help us look at, and deepen, our own faith, whatever it may be.

And as People of Faith, we can find unity amidst our diversity, companionship for our journey, respect for our common yearnings across the cultures, as well as stimulus and strength to work together for the future of our community.

Don't Discount The Role Of Religion

Faith and Religion:

Faith is trust in the Great Unknown, the Guiding Spirit, God by whatever name.
Religion is human attempts to define the indefinable

Faith is individual, experiential, a personal insight.
Religion is communal, organized, captured in tradition and codified on paper.

Faith can be a vital powerhouse for life.
Religion can be a pathway, or a roadblock, to the Great Divine.

Faith cannot be contained, can evolve, can escape religious boundaries.
Religion can channel its vision of the invisible and draw people to its vision.

Faith is amorphous, a "cloud of unknowing," an outreaching spirit.
Religion has many specific manifestations, touchstones that inspire the faithful.

Faith is hard to fight about.
Religions often have conflicts within and among them.

Faith shapes individuals.
Religions shape cultures and communities.

Faith can refer to many other things bedsides religion, i.e. faith in the government, in people, in promises, in YOU.
Religion can refer to the externals and the resulting cultures with little relationship to the actual faith of the affected people.

"Religious Faith" tries to combine the two.

Here in New Mexico we have two major religions, as well as many lesser ones.

Catholic: Ancient liturgies, long tradition, rich visual and audio beauty, comforting rituals, appeal to emotions, veneration of saints and remembrance of those who have gone before, mysticism, miracles, outreach to the poor and hungry, involvement of laity, authority from faraway Rome.

Protestant: Many mainstream varieties, from High Episcopal to Quaker. Bible based, much teaching and discussion of its messages. Independent interpretations. Appeal to intellect rather than emotions. Words and "*The Word*" important. Simple, unadorned surroundings (usually). Mission outreach, local and worldwide. Lay involvement. Some denominations "exclusionary," with lots of rules and regulations for membership. Others "inclusionary," welcoming everybody.

Hispanics: Tend to be Catholics for life, and much of the culture is bound up with the Catholic tradition.

Anglos: Tend to be Protestants, for as long as "the spirit moves them" and often move around from one Protestant organization to another.

Two very different approaches to religion and resulting cultural traditions. The boundaries are often hard to cross. Even the non-churched and atheists are affected by the religious cultures they inherit.

Each is rich is its own way.

Religious Perspectives

Puzzled Anglo:

"How strange these Hispanic Catholics are! Take for instance the Virgin of Guadalupe. She's venerated as the Patron Saint of Mexicans and New Mexicans. She's very special. Do you remember a while ago when an artist painted her picture in a bikini decorated with roses? What a brouhaha! Protests, marches, demonstrations, calls for the dismissal of the curator who had designed the exhibit. But at the same time she is depicted on low riders, t-shirts, tattoos . . . her picture even adorns the chest of a prizefighter. Is she there for protection, or to intimidate opponents? I wonder."

Puzzled Hispanic:

"These Protestant churches are so cold! They are so empty! Where are the statues of saints who bring color and warmth as they remind us of people like us who have celebrated God's power and brought God's love to us human beings? Where are images of Jesus on the cross where he suffered and died for us? Where are the candles whose flames bring specks of God's light in the darkness? Where is the scent of the incense that pervades everything like the Holy Spirit does? Where is Mother Mary who reaches out to us with her welcoming arms? How can Protestants feel the presence of God touching their lives in so many ways?"

New Identities

Years ago I was in charge of a program bringing together a Trappist monk, a Sufi, and a Buddhist for an inter-religious dialogue. I was surprised by the fact that each had come from a different religious tradition. The monk had grown up a Pentecostal and cherished the ancient ritual and silence of the monastic life. The Sufi had been a Jewish boy and delighted in the Sufi parable-like storytelling practice. The Buddhist had been an Episcopalian. He particularly appreciated the silent meditation without the distractions of liturgy. Each of them had utterly rejected their original religious heritage and also been shaped by it, adopting or transforming elements of the faith. As converts, they were particularly knowledgeable and enthusiastic and gave us a fascinating evening. Yet, I was saddened that each had known so little about his original faith that they sought in other traditions what they had missed in their own.

Music Hath Charms

One time we *Vecinos* planned an interfaith music evening. The room was overcrowded, hot and stuffy, but nobody left. The members of the choir from one of our Hispanic Catholic churches huddled together warily, shy and nervous among so many Anglos.

The Cantor from our major Jewish temple at that time was a woman with a lovely voice and a warm, outgoing presence. She explained the backgrounds of the Jewish liturgical music she shared, with humor and details that fascinated us non-Jewish folks.

The Methodist choir director was also a woman. She led us through some of the old Gospel hymns with an enthusiasm that would have shaken the rafters if there had been any rafters to shake.

The Presbyterian 'Band' was a lively bunch of old folks. One played the piano, another a fiddle, a third an accordion, backed up by a harmonica, a washtub, maracas and bongos. They swung into a series of familiar folk-rock hymns, encouraging us all to join in when we could. Their patter between the songs was hilarious and kept us all laughing.

At last, it was the turn of the Hispanic choir. The twelve or fifteen members, of all ages, seemed nervous at first, but soon calmed down. They played a couple of guitars and an accordion and had fine voices. They passed out song sheets with the Spanish words to songs, some of which were lively, and some less familiar Spanish traditional. A special warmth and joy radiated from them that totally captivated all us Anglos present, and we urged them to continue long after they thought they had finished.

Then—refreshments, mingling, conversations. The harmonica player from the Band came over to me with his arm around one of the Hispanic girls. "Anita here lives two houses away from me and I never even said hello to her. That'll change."

And it did. For the next couple of years, the Band frequently played at the Catholic church and the Hispanic choir enlivened many Presbyterian services, while the mingling and relationships continued. They only terminated when age and frailty finally caused the Band to disband.

More Values To Consider

As the Fourth of July approached, articles in newspapers and magazines pondered, "Who Are We, Citizens of the USA?" and "What Is The Current

Intercultural Emphasis Saying to Us?" How can we balance our Unity with our Diversity?

These articles have challenged me to think more deeply about what I mean when I use the term *multicultural* as an ideal, and what is the role of *Vecinos* when we promote "multicultural community" in Santa Fe.

It seems to me that many extremists of both ends of the spectrum distort both the realities and the ideal.

On the one hand, many celebrate the melting pot, the opportunity for people from everywhere to abandon their roots and remake themselves in a new image. Surely, this is part of the picture and has brought happiness and success to generations of immigrant families.

On the other hand come cries from the many who have not "melted" in the pot. People whose roots go deep in the land, whose cultural heritage defines them, who have never been stirred into the national pot. And people who have "escaped." People who in their search for their own affirmation and dignity reject outright many of the values and practices of the mainstream. People whose cultures or values have been exploited, disparaged, isolated for generations.

For me, the realities lie somewhere in the middle as I try to combine a respect for all cultural strands and seek a unity of perspective and purpose within the larger whole.

Rather than a "melting pot" that squeezes everybody into one bland blend, I favor the stew pot image where the intact cultural carrots and potatoes, meat and onions in a savory gravy can enrich the whole feast.

As *Vecinos* continues to pull together people across the cultures for talk and sharing and developing relationships, it seems to me that we need to consider three basic areas.

1. What is this modern American culture that we both celebrate and revile? The basic principles on which it was built still serve as a magnet for displaced and depressed people from all over the world. In spite of abuses and distortions we can all condemn, the promise still holds. The

traditional "Life, liberty and the Pursuit of Happiness . . . and Justice for All," however interpreted, still sounds pretty good. But, whether you are a New England Yankee or a kid from Cochiti Pueblo, the grandson of German immigrants or a descendant of Don Pedro de Peralta, how do we interpret and claim this promise for ourselves? Not with guilt trips, not with copouts, not with uncritical acquiescence—but standing firmly on our feet.

2. How can many of us live in two worlds? The mainstream culture is not going to go away: it's the context in which we live and have our being. We all have to learn to understand it and to cope with its demands and opportunities. BUT not at the expense of our own heritage. Whether we are Comanche or Jewish, Mexican or Tibetan, we need to claim our own roots with pride and compassion and understanding of our basic values. We only have something to offer this wider whole when we accept and understand our own vari-cultured selves. The ongoing dialogue between our different perspectives creates both tension and opportunity. There are many ways of dealing with this: let's find them.

3. There is much that each of us can learn from deep contact with other cultures. Whether it is new perspectives on our own culture or new ways of seeing and doing, it can help us break the bonds of cultural isolationism, so we can work together for our own community as well as for our wider world.

10

Communications

*W*e say what we mean and mean what we say. Don't we? Well, yes and no.

Words And Feathers

*F*or some of us words are all important. Spoken or written they convey our questions and information, our hopes and experiences, our heritage and our values. They come along in neat progression, one at a time, building up a picture step by logical step. Words are solid, definite, dependable, in the dictionary.

For others, words are just words. *Palabras y plumas, el viento las lleva,* as the old proverb warns us. "Words and feathers, the wind blows them away." Much more important than the words alone are the non-verbal clues that "word people" often dismiss entirely.

Who are the people involved in the conversation? Are they strangers or friends, with reputations or relationships? What is the context of the conversation? Is it friendly and relaxed, or serious with an open or hidden agenda?

Cultural expectations and experience affect the ways we communicate, or fail to. It's really hard to hear what someone is saying when it doesn't match the expected stereotype. Certain words, while representing a common experience in one culture, cause only puzzlement in another, or bring communications to a screeching halt. I call these latter "bug words," because they "bug" people.

Humor, what's considered funny, can often bring people together in wonderful ways, but just as often can backfire into unexpected conflicts or misunderstandings.

Conflict is inevitable in a diverse, multicultural community like ours. Different perspectives, cultural experiences, visions for our future and strategies for working toward these visions often clash. Yet conflicts can clarify situations rather than destroy them.

We can learn to communicate with each other across the cultures, in depth, with good humor and delight. But it takes time, sensitivity, ability to listen and willingness to keep trying.

Complexities

Communication is a complex process in the best of circumstances. It involves not only the message we believe we have sent, but also the message that has been received. Sometimes they are quite different. Nothing is as simple as the old idea that "I say what I mean and I mean what I say."

Cross-cultural communications can be distorted by stereotypes, conflicting values, cultural and personal experiences, communication styles, and ways of doing things. We seldom talk about these areas and therefore barely understand them.

How can we learn to listen to each other more effectively, to really hear what the others are trying to tell us? How can we make sure that the message we are sending is the one received?

One of the most helpful concepts, for me, came from a Chinese psychologist at a very tense point in a Black-White race relations conference in the 1960s.

He reminded us that we listen to each other on three basic levels: head, heart and gut. We need to be aware of these levels as we send and receive messages and try to figure out what is meant as well as what is said.

"Head" is the rational, objective level, where words are understood literally and language is expected to mean what it says. It involves factual descriptions of things, ideas, events, experiences, desires, plans where there should be no confusion. Many of us work consciously only on this level.

"Heart" is the relationship level, where we express our good will—or lack thereof—toward others. We try to see the person in context, to listen with patience to more than the words expressed. "Heart listening" takes time and develops the relationship within which real communication can emerge.

"Gut" is the feeling level, deeper than words. It often erupts in emotional explosions or actions. It can be very powerful in either the positive or negative aspects, and it must be recognized and respected as a legitimate element in all our communications.

Much of our communications confusion comes from crisscrossing these three levels. For instance, a person operating on the head level can lose patience with someone operating at the heart level, who is concerned with relationships and doesn't necessarily stick to the agenda. On the other hand, a head person may seem cold and uncaring to the heart person. (This is often a major problem in meetings between agenda-focused Anglos and relationship-focused Hispanics.)

Someone exploding at the gut level can strike terror in the head people because such emotions destroy rational discourse. Yet such explosions are often the only way to make people pay attention to the issues and the feelings of others.

Bug Words

These are common words that have different resonances across the cultures and can cause communications to come to a screeching halt. Here are some examples:

At a large *Vecinos* meeting some time ago, one of the Hispanics present spoke up about "institutional racism." Although this is part of the common experience of many Hispanics, it is not something that most Anglos, as part of the "dominant" culture, have experienced. A conscientious observer (my video cam) could notice the unconscious stiffening of Anglo bodies and the little red flags flapping wildly. "No, not me! I'm not involved!" They seemed to be saying, "Let's not pursue the subject."

A little later at the same meeting, one of the panelists, sensing the rising tension and trying to be conciliatory, admonished, "Calm down, folks. Remember, we're all Americans here!" His intentions were the best, attempting to draw all present into the inclusive "American Dream" and to assure everybody that they were valued and respected as part of our national community. But almost every Hispanic body in the room tensed up. The same proverbial little red flags flapped briskly, the same kind of tuning out became evident. For many of the Hispanics present, the "American Dream" had been exclusionary, a place of prejudice and discrimination, and of alien values that have never really claimed them.

Two well-meaning individuals, each unaware of how words expressing their cultural experience could "bug" other people across the cultures and sidetrack discussions important to us all.

Bug Words are everywhere. Our ideas are important to us. We tend to take our interpretations for granted. When other people express different perspectives, we sometimes get defensive. *"What are you talking about? I know what this means! You're wrong!"* And communication comes to a screeching halt. Or we ignore both the speaker and the alternative interpretation, leaving them both in a fuzzy limbo.

This is a time to stop and listen. To show respect for alternative points of view. To explore the deeper meanings for all concerned. To re-think and to re-phrase the topic to mutual satisfaction. Yes, it takes time and patience, but it can be part of an ongoing process.

Communications Confusions: How To Resolve Them

First, we can recognize that confusions exist. We can remember that we are NOT all alike, that other people, even within our own culture, have many different perceptions of reality as we see it. Communication with each other is not as simple as we think.

Second, we can try to see though the 'easy stereotypes' to the lives of real people. We can learn enough about the heritage to understand the backgrounds. We can think about our own perspectives and experiences and see how they interrelate with the others.

Third, we can use words with care. Of course, we make blunders. "Bug words" slip out. We goof up caring conversations in ways we could not imagine. This is where a sense of humor is essential, where we can laugh together at our misstatements. Listening and learning go together in a constant dialogue.

Fourth, when it seems that our message is not getting across, rephrase it, restate it, explain it. When we don't understand the message we're receiving, ask about its meaning. These may seem simplistic, but many people, including us, sometimes really do not understand. Stop and clarify before confusion leads to disaster.

Most of us approach each other across the cultures warily, with hope and good intentions. We must be careful to show respect and consideration for each other and attempt to really hear what is being said. It isn't always easy. But don't let important ideas or information to be distorted by our intercultural communications blunders.

Of course, there are some people who will tell you what they think you want to hear whether or not it is true.

Or others who have been lied to and exploited by outsiders until they are wary of speaking openly to you, if at all, with you.

Some will want to exploit you for their own advantage, and there may be some you will want to exploit yourself.

Others, who are superficially polite, may be full of unresolved anger that may leap out in unexpected ways, devastating the unsuspecting victim (you and me).

And a few who will outright lie to you for self-protection, if anxious, or to lure you away when your questions become intrusive.

But these are exceptions and they may be found in every heritage, including our own.

What can we do in such situations? Keep our cool. Don't give way to anger or stereotypes. Look at the larger context as much as we understand it. Try to sort out the *what* and the *why* of what is being said—or not. And listen, with head, heart and gut.

Voices

"How can we do research and not ask questions? Our academic colleagues think we're crazy. They want to know everything in a hurry and they rush through long lists of questions according to their specialties. But for many of our Pueblo and Hispanic neighbors direct questions are intrusive, rude, and tend to shut off developing relationships. Trust has so often been abused by Anglo visitors who made friends with local people, quizzed them intensively, went home as "experts", wrote books and articles that distorted and sensationalized and took out of context what they had heard. And they made money. So direct questions are often met with stony silence, outright fabrications, jokes or sassy comments to move away from the theme. Yet as we try to meet New Mexicans on their own terms, we've come to know well many families, and we've found that by taking time to be with them, keeping our mouths shut and our eyes and ears open, we've been able to learn what we want to know in an atmosphere of trust and caring. It takes time and patience and genuine interest to develop the friendships that will allow real conversations about the things we are researching, on a much deeper level than if we were simply asking questions. And it's essential never to abuse confidences even when we don't know they are confidential."
—Wise professor

❖❖❖

"Pueblo children generally don't ask questions. They are taught to look and listen and become aware of all things going on around them, from the moods of their elders to the rituals of the dances. When they get into the Anglo school system width its high priority on verbal questions and answers, where they are expected to ask when they don't understand and offer ideas and responses, many of them have problems."
—Teacher at Santa Fe Indian School

❖❖❖

"If you think standing around on street corners and chitchatting with your neighbors is a waste of time, then you'll have real trouble learning to communicate with many of our New Mexicans."
—Veteran Observer

❖❖❖

"For us Anglos, the power lies in the pen. We articulate, verbal, literate people become the leaders, the moderators of group meetings, the information disseminators, the action interpreters, the sharer of dreams. We want to capture everything, imprison ideas with words and use their power to make changes. People of other cultures whose powers are not necessarily written-verbal feel squeezed out of Anglo-dominated meetings. We Anglos don't know how to listen to them, to use the gifts they have to offer. We're puzzled and frustrated when all the non-Anglos disappear from our pet projects."
—Carol

❖❖❖

"Why do these Anglo folks come rushing in here with solutions before they even know what the problems are? Some of them could be so helpful! How can we teach them to look, listen and learn before they try to change things?"
—Hispanic activist

❖❖❖

A Navajo woman was in charge of one of our meetings. When she saw the chairs lined up in the usual straight lines, she protested. Let's move the chairs," she directed. "Make a big circle or horseshoe. We have to be able to see each other, to see who's talking, to watch reactions and expressions. To look as well as to listen to the words. We're together, we're a community. We're not just a bunch of isolated individuals. We're here to consider the words and wisdom of our presenter and to share our observations with all of us. This is the Indian way, and it is good."
—Navajo leader

❖❖❖

"I worked for years with my people in churches and community programs, and everybody seemed pleased with my style and my relationships with them. Then I went away for a while to work in an Anglo community. There I learned the Anglo way of doing things and got pretty good at it. When I came home to Santa Fe, I wanted to teach my people the new ways I had

learned. But do you know what? They didn't work. Not here. And bit by bit, I had to learn all over again the practices I had forgotten or discarded before I could begin to work creatively with my people again. They say that what works elsewhere does not work in New Mexico. I guess this is an example."
—Veteran church worker

About Lucy

In meetings, generally Anglos concentrate on the task to be accomplished, while for Hispanics and Indians the people involved are more important. Anglos think in a linear fashion, with one thing leading to another in a logical progression. Hispanics and Indians tend to think contextually, seeing background and multiple ramifications as integral parts of the topic at hand. Anglos use words sparingly, to present an argument or to make a point. Hispanics and Indians use words liberally to create a multidimensional picture. Anglos feel appreciated for their ideas; Hispanics and Indians feel appreciated for the quality of their personalities.

Lucy, who at that time was an intercultural conflict mediator, often told this story.

She had been called in to the final meeting of a Task Force that had been gathering at intervals for about a year. Made up of county and tribal leaders, the task force was to develop a series of guidelines for sorting out the overlapping jurisdictions of tribal and county governments, an overlap that had been creating constant conflict and confusion throughout their area. The task force had been getting nowhere. The minutes showed meeting after meeting breaking up in frustration, with nothing accomplished. Many of the original task force members had quit in discouragement. And the final report was due to the National Association of Counties.

When Lucy walked into the room, she saw a dozen tired, frustrated, hostile individuals. Though they were scheduled for a two-day session, they were ready to give up and go home. Now. What could she, an experienced mediator, bring to them in this seemingly hopeless situation?

Curious about the people and stalling for time and inspiration, Lucy asked the group members to tell her a bit about themselves. "I assume you all know each other pretty well, since you've been meeting so often," she commented. "But I don't know you at all. Please start at this end of the room."

The first two or three of the task force to speak were Anglo men. "My name is so-and-so; I own a gas station in such-and-such a town, and I'm the county sheriff . . ." "I'm so-and-so and I'm a construction engineer, I live in this town . . ." Basic facts, that's all.

The fourth person was a middle-aged Navajo woman from a small place on the Navajo reservation. She gave her name, but that was not all. She continued with her clans and those of her parents and grandparents, and started talking about her life on the reservation. She described her parents, the hogan she lived in, what it was like to herd sheep. She recalled how it felt to be shipped off to a BIA boarding school when she was young, about the education she got there, about the college she attended as one of the few Navajos from her area. She talked about her return to the reservation, her struggles to make a living, her gradual involvement in tribal politics. She spoke of relations with the Anglo bureaucracy, her feelings when she walked into a room full of Anglo politicians as the lone Navajo and a woman at that. She talked of her hopes for her people, and what she wanted to accomplish through this particular task force. She went on and on, for a good twenty minutes, laying out her life, her experience, her hopes. Lucy expected any one of the men to leap up and protest that this long description had nothing to do with the reason they were there, that it was time to get down to business. But nobody moved, all apparently caught up in the woman's tale.

Though the other Anglos provided minimal information, each of the other Navajos told their stories too. And everybody listened!

Though it was almost lunchtime when the introductions were finished, Lucy invited, "We've learned quite a lot about some of our members here, but not so much about others. Do you want to go around again and tell us more?" They did. Although the Anglos tried, and they were less comfortable talking about themselves, a deeper picture of each of them as individuals began to emerge.

Lunch was animated, congenial in a way several people told Lucy had never happened before. And when the group reconvened afterwards, suddenly everybody was eager to talk business. The ideas expressed were being heard with a new openness. As the afternoon went on, everything began to come together, and by the end of the second day, the task force had produced together a document all could be proud of.

Lucy commented that the task force members had never listened to each other as people. They had seen each other as "positions" represented by people, rather than as people who happened to represent "positions." The switch in perceptions made a crucial difference. Negotiations among people were possible in a way that concentration on positions could not allow.

Vexes And Values

"VEXES" inhibit intercultural communications. "VALUES" enhance intercultural communications. Examples:

Vex: You insist that intercultural communications are no problem. We speak the same language. Words mean the same thing everywhere.
Value: You know that communications are complex. Words often have many interpretations in different cultures.

Vex: We stereotype everything and everybody—the easy way.
Value: We smash stereotypes—see individuals and situations instead.

Vex: We assume "dominant" mainstream culture to be correct.
Value: We know different cultural experiences challenge "correctness."

Vex: Words mean what they say.
Value: Words often disguise what they mean.

Vex: We expect quick solutions to problems
Value: We give time for solutions to ripen.

Vex: You expect people to come to you.
Value: You go where people are.

Vex: You use "bug words" frequently.
Value: You recognize when words "bug" people.

Vex: You fear making mistakes, don't try.
Value: You anticipate mistakes, learn from them.

Vex: You talk, don't listen.
Value: You listen more than talk.

Vex: You expect dominant values are true for everybody.
Value: You know values vary and often conflict.

Vex: You expect people to respect you.
Value: You let them know you respect them.

Vex: You expect the worst.
Value: You look for the best.

Vex: You keep past history and grievances current.
Value: You acknowledge the past, but let it stay in the past.

Vex: You are uptight and overly serious in multicultural situations.
Value: You can relax, relate, enjoy, enrich.

Vex: You say nothing when people disparage others.
Value: You try to interpret people to each other.

Vex: You hear words only.
Value: You hear words, context, emotions with your heart, as well as your head.

Why?

Frequent cries rend the air. "Why aren't there more Hispanics at our Anglo meetings? After all, we're trying to help them as well as the rest of us? "How can we involve the Indians?" "Why can't the Anglos see how they discourage us?" "Doesn't anybody care?"

Of course people care—about issues important to them. But here are some things to remember:

Lifelong residents of the area often have complicated webs of responsibilities to extended families, churches, tribal and community organizations. When they also have to work two or more jobs for mere survival, their time and energy are limited for all but the most critical and immediate concerns. In contrast, many of the "activists" are Anglo newcomers with adequate incomes and a minimum of longstanding responsibilities.

Those whose cultures and concerns have been overridden over the years are often discouraged, pessimistic and bitter. Generally, the newcomers to the area are the energetic optimists. Offering new hope and vision is a difficult task, and credibility is often an essential issue. Trust does not develop overnight.

So many projects, visions, and leaders come and go that many people hesitate to spend their time and energies on something that will quickly disappear. They need to watch and listen for a long time, maybe years, before they are willing to join in.

Meetings just to get acquainted hold little interest for over-committed folks. But those that deal with practical matters that affect their children, their housing, their jobs, their communities are more likely to get a response.

The styles of meetings are important also. Task-oriented Anglo-style meetings with formal agendas and lots of paper intimidate (or bore) some folks, while those with a lot of people-contacts make others "antsy." There needs to be some combination to make people feel welcome and also to get the work done. Some people can do this easily, but for others the balance is very difficult.

"Get acquainted" times are important, yes, but they are just the beginning. Follow-ups can include sharing concerns, alliances, assistance, resources that can make a difference for individuals and people involved. But building relationships is the first essential step.

This Was One Of The Many Times I Felt I Had Really Goofed

Church Rock Navajos were worried about their water supply that had been contaminated by uranium tailings from a nearby mine. Concerned people at the New Mexico Council of Churches had arranged for some nuclear scientists from New York to address their concerns. Who can argue with the latest hard science rather than rumor and suspicions? The analysis of the water supplies had already been done, though the scientists had not yet seen the results before the appointed day.

I was simply an observer and had driven from Santa Fe with three or four concerned Anglos for the event. We met at one of the chapter houses where Navajos were gathering. Some thirty or forty of them were already sitting around the edges of the large meeting hall, watching and waiting, while more filtered in. As we entered they looked at us with hope and curiosity, shifting in their chairs, the better to observe us interesting strangers.

Normally I'm quite comfortable in intercultural situations. But this time I wasn't. Confronted by all those brown faces, inexplicably I panicked and rushed to join the other Anglos marching across the room. I could easily have circled the room, greeting and shaking hands with each individual as my ignored instinct insisted. But I didn't. If I had, we—the Navajos and I—might have felt connected, sharing a mutual interest, recognizing in each other our common humanity. No, it wouldn't have affected the outcome of the meeting, but it might have altered the tone. Other overtures I later tried to make were just too late. I was branded as just one of the ignorant Anglos from elsewhere.

The scientists arrived, dressed in their city suits and ties. They were young men, friends of somebody who had cajoled them into this trip. They looked scared and nervous. The hall filled up and the meeting began. Long introductions filled much of what was left of the morning—of who we Anglos were and why we had come, and of the Navajos and their concerns about their water. The young Navajo interpreter was magnificent! He not only translated the words and ideas expressed, but he also filled in the context for both the Navajos and us with background information about our cultures and expectations for this meeting. He was good! But this naturally took a lot of time, and I could see the scientists were restless, while the Navajos listened intently.

Meanwhile, some women had killed a sheep and were cooking it in a huge pot over a fire outside the door. I watched them for a bit. Though they stoked the fire with more wood constantly, it never heated the water to a proper boil. I tried to look friendly and used both my English and basic Spanish with no response. The cultural gulf was too wide. Eventually, they served us platters of watery soup. Mine had an onion floating in it and a sheep rib so tough my teeth could barely pull off a fragment of meat. The New York scientists weren't hungry.

My discomforts were nothing compared with those of the scientists. They had never been away from New York and knew nothing about the reservation and its people. They had flown into Gallup that morning. They had scorched their mouths on chile at breakfast. They had studied the analysis of the water samples. Their host had taken then to see the streams and springs the samples had come from. They were shocked! They had never seen land that to them seemed so desolate. They had never seen people living in such poverty. They had never imagined the distances between hogans and services—such as they were. They knew nothing about Navajos or their way of life. The water, they insisted, was so full of contaminants of every sort that any uranium residue was irrelevant. By rights, long ago, that water should have killed all people and livestock using it for miles around.

They didn't know how to say this politely to their waiting listeners. The first speaker resorted to a lot of technical detail about the analysis of the water with so much jargon that nobody understood what he was talking about. The second tried to explain the necessity of a source of clean water, but he had no suggestions of where to find a clean source nor how to clean up the water they actually had available. The third one focused on health measures, clearly out of his depth and talking as if his hearers were ignorant children. Then he mentioned that at home they all drank Perrier Water that had been imported in bottles from France, and which contains traces of radioactivity, which is "good for you." He offered to send some cases of it for the Navajos to try, and if they liked it they could buy it for everybody.

Whew! Talk about cultural gulfs! Perrier Water? I didn't know whether to laugh or to cry, so I did some of both.

One of the Navajo elders then spoke at length, thanking the outsiders for coming so far from their homes to the meeting, and for caring about the plight of the Navajos. But, to put it bluntly, they hadn't been much help. The other Navajos laughed and cheered, echoing his words. The scientists were antsy, eager to be off to catch their plane and return to their familiar civilization. I felt sad for them and wanted to speak with them, but they dashed off too quickly. The organizers (not me) huddled in a little group wondering what had happened.

The best of intentions had gone astray. It was a mistake to bring in those poor scientists with no understanding of the realities of Navajo life. It was not helpful to raise the expectations among the Navajos that the scientists would have something of value to offer. The event had much to teach us all, if we cared to listen. And I was wondering, as I still do, what I might have done to mitigate the situation .Probably nothing. But I still wonder.

❖ *11* ❖

Racism

*R*acism takes on many different shapes and degrees of intensity. Though it is frequently cited it is seldom defined. We can't even begin to deal with racism in our communities until we know what we are talking about. Each type of racism requires different levels of response. Racism is as much an attitude as an action.

A Reality

"*R*acism" is an ugly word. Hurled like a grenade, it shatters institutions, communities, relationships. Shouted as a war cry, it raises anger, fear, threats of violence. Coldly calculated, it throws up barriers to opportunity, to communications, to justice. Lurking just below the surface of many intercultural situations, it threatens to pounce on caring individuals and to attack good intentions. Simmering in the depths of community and personal consciousness, it provides for some people an excuse for failure, for others a spur to creative action. It's a reality that some people suffer, others fight; some nurture and others ignore. Racism as a general term includes more than skin color. Heritage, language, religion, gender, lifestyle, and more, are aspects used as a basis for general discrimination.

Racism, actual or perceived, is a harsh reality for countless people. Deliberate, incidental or accidental, it hurts victims and perpetrators alike. It creates gulfs instead of bridges, exclusion rather than community, and denies the rich diversity of perspectives and experiences in our shared business of living.

It is often convenient to forget that racism affects people in almost all cultures, that few of us, of whatever heritage, are free of stereotypes and prejudices about "others." Racism is just as misleading when it is positive—"So-and-so can do no wrong"—as when it is negative—"So-and-so can do no right"—and when desire for "racial balance" overrides the capacity of individuals involved.

Let's take a look at some of the common types of racism we frequently encounter.

Hard-Core Racism

This is a strong prejudice against certain kinds of people. It's based on emotion, conviction, experience, history, religion, hearsay, economics, sex, fear, tradition. There's an impulse to defend turf, jobs, neighborhoods, family "purity" and institutions from those "outsiders." A heavy reliance on stereotypes, both negative and positive, is involved, as are efforts to force individuals into "boxes." It's displayed through racist jokes and stories, exclusion, disparagement, laws, fights, and sometimes violence by hate groups that maim and kill.

How can we deal with this kind of racism? Sometimes we can't. It involves too much gut-level emotion, defensiveness, selective "justification," and resistance to change. New laws can enforce compliance as in the Civil Rights South, as can community pressure. Change comes slowly in spite of resistance. One persistent, persuasive voice can sometimes make a difference—think of Martin Luther King or Cesar Chavez.

Racial Profiling

Negative stereotypes of strangers based on color of skin, clothing, companions, accessories and actions. Often used by police, bystanders, and nervous neighbors. Seen as signals of potential danger—as gangs, armed thugs, drunks, possible thieves arouse anxiety—which may or may not be valid. Sometimes the anxiety can be justified, as newspapers report instances of violence or abuse. But most of the time those profiled are peacefully going about their business.

Don't panic. Look at the threats as people, as individuals, not frightening stereotypes, and let them know you see them. It may or may not help. But the climate of fear that develops, overreaction by the authorities, vulnerability of the citizens, nervousness about unfamiliar color and culture, are all aspects of our community we need to address.

Institutional Racism

Official policy, custom or quotas lead an organization to exclude admittance or restrict participation for targeted groups. Although seldom admitted, the reality of exclusion is felt by hundreds of people on the basis of race alone. "No Negroes admitted, Indians stay out, you brown-skinned Hispanics don't need to apply." "Yes, you can do donkey work, but don't come near the offices." "We know you have worked here for years but we don't want to listen to your ideas." "No Hispanic has ever gone to this school. Whites only." Glass ceilings everywhere.

How can we deal with this situation? Recognize that changes are happening, slowly. It's significant that now we can see black, brown and red national newscasters, musicians, business folks, teachers, along with the predominant White ones. Politicians and community leaders, particularly in New Mexico, come from many backgrounds. Community pressure, particularly where money is involved, can remedy many situations. But the politics of exclusion are hard to fight.

Interracial Discomfort

People who are different from ourselves and unfamiliar often cause high anxiety levels. We don't know how to act with others, how to talk with them, what to expect. We have heard too many stereotypes or stories of racial conflicts past and recent. We're wary of the unknown, insecure in our responses, afraid of rejection or exploitation, reluctant to take the initiative, wondering why bother? A black face, a brown one, or a white one may leave us tongue-tied.

This is where contact, in either natural or contrived situations, can make a difference. Sometimes a guide or interpreter—or class—can open the way. With kids at the park, a shared experience, food at the Farmers' Market, a dance on the Plaza, a hike in the hills . . . or a neighborhood meeting about an issue important to all can start conversations. Individual connections can start to break down stereotypes and increase comfort. And always remember that the other person may also be afraid of you.

Unintended Racism

We all goof occasionally. We display our ignorance in unfamiliar situations, or say something insensitive, or manage to "mis-speak" when we don't realize it. Maybe we hadn't considered enough about what we were thinking, doing or saying. Perhaps the context has confused us and something stupid has leaked out. This is a common experience, even for us with the best of intentions.

What do we need to do? Lighten up! Remember that our goofups are not unique to us. We need to look at the larger context and the obvious intentions and learn and laugh with each other about our "stupid mistakes." They are inevitable, so get used to them, and move on.

Misperceived Racism

Some people are highly "oversensitive" and, based on experience, may see "racist" remarks or actions where none are intended. And they label you as "racist" and spread the word and initiate innuendoes against you that undermine your credibility. It's not fun.

What can one do? Here again, context, intentions, communications and time will help sort out the real from the misperceived racism and help heal the rift.

Internalized Racism

Some people reject their own heritage on racist grounds. They feel intense shame that forbears fostered slavery, or rode with the KKK, or exterminated Native people or destroyed the environment, or lived in shiftless poverty . . . or whatever. They try to disassociate themselves from their own heritage and identify themselves with one they feel is more congenial, which usually doesn't really accept them. Many sad people are the result.

What can we say? Most races/cultures have good and bad elements. When a person, voluntarily or not, focuses exclusively on one or another aspect, the necessary balance is disrupted. Often the person is left off-balance too. Only by accepting one's race, gender, culture, heritage, with all their complexities, can an individual meet the world as a whole person.

How Can We Fight Racism In Our Community?

Lots of suggestions are embedded in these pages. Everything we have been considering may reflect our pervasive racism. Think about the many possibilities, from eliminating stereotypes to improving communications.

We can be sparing with the word "racism." It's one of those "bug words" that can create either emotional explosions or denial, and disrupt communication. There are many other ways to express the effects of racism. Figure them out and use them.

Also, we can be specific about what we are describing. A person is "racist"; an organization practices "institutional racism"; that leader makes racist remarks." Not enough. Details, please, break the generalities down to specifics. Then maybe—just maybe—we can find solutions.

It's only "racism" when it disparages, belittles, excludes, harms or denies opportunity to another person. It's the intention, perceived or actual, that causes the problem. Though ignorance is another factor, it can be remedied by education or creative contact.

Just because you are uncomfortable in an alien culture, with unknown people, it does not mean you are a "racist."

Voices

"Those big Anglos don't even see us smaller Hispanics. On the streets, in the stores, in lines, they usually look right over us or past us as if we weren't even there. Their attitudes say, since we're invisible we don't exist. It hurts and adds to our feelings of anger at those unfeeling Anglos. We don't generally have the courage to step up and say, 'We're here. We're next. Look at us.' Maybe that's what we need to do."
—A small, hurting Hispanic woman

❖❖❖

"I grew up in Kansas, in a small town where everybody looked the same, all White, hardworking farm and town people. It was a friendly and comfortable place. Then I moved to Santa Fe where I'm surrounded by all these different kinds of people, of all colors and backgrounds. I can't understand what they say when they look at me. It's scary. I don't know how to act or how to think about them. Racism is everywhere. I didn't think I was one, but I'm afraid I've become a racist here."
—An anxious newcomer

❖❖❖

"I'm Mexican and I look it. I've lived here for thirty years, I'm an American citizen and I own my own business. But I've been arrested twice while I was peacefully going about my errands. The cop thought I looked "suspicious" and that was all he needed. I was released after a few hours in jail, no real damage was done. But now, whenever a cop looks at me I shrivel inside."
—A Mexican carpenter

❖❖❖

Years ago, a teacher stood me up in front of our fourth grade class beside a blue-eyed, golden-haired Anglo girl. She told the class that this brown-skinned boy would never make it, was sure to be a failure, perhaps a criminal. The girl, on the other hand, was sure to be a great success at whatever she attempted. For years, I've been trying to overcome this terrible image of myself as someone doomed from the start. I graduated from the University of New Mexico, I'm self-supporting, I have my own business. I'm contributing to the community in many ways. I help with my church's outreach programs to the hungry and shut-ins. I'm raising a fine family. I'm not ashamed of what I've accomplished in spite of myself. The last I heard of the golden-haired girl is that she IS a success. She's a famous prostitute and owns the most elegant bordello in Albuquerque."

—A local businessman

And Vistas

An Anglo friend, a young man who has recorded folk music all over the area and seemed quite comfortable in intercultural situations asked where I was going. I described a family gathering where some community plans would be discussed, a gathering that probably would be predominantly Hispanic. "Why don't you come along?" I invited. He seemed reluctant, even though he was looking for something to do. At last he admitted, "I don't want to go to a Hispanic meeting because I'm afraid I might find out that I'm a racist and that's not how I want to see myself."

❖ ❖ ❖

A Sioux friend had a job driving a Senior Citizen van for the city. He was always careful and friendly with his charges, and they seemed to like him, giving him good reports. One day one of his passengers, a little old lady, had trouble getting out of the van and staggered on reaching the sidewalk. My friend, ever helpful, took her arm and steadied her as they approached the desired doorway. A little later he was called to the office. He was fired. The little old lady, irate, had complained to the authorities that that "disgusting Indian" had actually touched her and she demanded his dismissal. No hearing, no redress. My friend was simply out of a job he liked.

Rafe

The year was 1965. The place New Hampshire. It seems a long way from Santa Fe in 2013, but the experience there taught me things important for all my intercultural/interracial contacts ever since.

The Civil Rights Movement was still young. Blacks and Whites were unsure of how to relate to each other. About a hundred people, Blacks and Whites and their families, had gathered on the shore of Lake Winnepesaukee for a weeklong conference on Race Relations that was sponsored by the New England Council of Churches. It was a first.

We were very tentative with each other, trying so hard not to make any racial "boo-boos" that inevitably we did. My husband, for instance, let loose such comments as, "That's mighty white of you" to a Black woman passing the bread, and "I worked till I was black in the face" in another situation. When I saw my eight-year-old son and a Black boy rolling on the ground trying to kill each other, my heart sank. It turned out that the mêlée was about a dropped camera and had nothing to do with race.

All of us were very polite with each other, keeping comments superficial and retreating back to "our own kind" for affirmation. Dutifully, we followed the programs and discussions as organized by the staff who were treading new territory, as we all were. Everything was going smoothly until about the fourth day—when all HELL broke loose.

The setting was a role play in which White volunteers representing Black ones and vice versa were discussing "plans" to meet some common need. All low key and interesting. Suddenly, a voice from the back of the room started shouting.

"That's not the way it is! How can you Whites pretend to be Black? You don't know nothing about it. You're just a bunch of phony liberals who pretend to be enlightened, but don't know BEANS! You're oppressors, you're exploiters, just like the worst of them! And you Blacks here are just as bad as the Whites! You're a bunch of Uncle Toms! Oreos!"

"Shouting" is too tame a word: the man was roaring.

Rafe was a short, stocky, very black preacher from somewhere in Connecticut. His rage was real. A lifetime of anger, frustration, injustice, and racial hatred spilled out of him. His charges cut to the quick everyone who heard him. Here we were, all of us, trying to work on reconciliation, seeking ways to make our ideals and our efforts count for something, to promote civil rights for all. The leaders and many others tried to reason with him, to shout back, to calm him down, which resulted in more tirades, more anger, more charges, more fury that lashed and battered all of us present.

The meeting broke up soon, and that afternoon and evening were miserable times of soul-searching for most of us. We sat by ourselves on the beach wrapped in our own painful introspections. We talked soberly in small groups. The mood was so low we couldn't even play with our puzzled kids. If Rafe was right and we were a bunch of phony liberals coming together only so that we could feel good about ourselves without any real involvement in things that might make a difference, that was a very harsh revelation. As we struggled with our inner turmoil, the Conference was on the verge of breaking up, along with our shattered self-images.

The next day a psychologist started to put us back together again. He was Chinese. As an objective observer, he could relate to both Blacks and Whites. Rafe's outburst, he assured us, was the first "genuine" thing that had happened during the days we had been there. He reminded us that there are three levels of communication. At the head level most of our previous discussions had taken place. The heart level represented the good will that had brought us all here together. The gut level was what had spilled out of Rafe. The Head level and the Gut level do not connect. Over the next hour, he tried to help us hear what Rafe was trying to communicate through his visceral rage, asking Rafe to move his roars up to the head level, and the rest of us to move our ears to the gut. It was hard to do and involved us all. Rafe still roared, the rest of us still shuddered, but we began to learn to listen. Throughout the rest of the week we kept asking each other, "Are you speaking from head, heart or gut?"

These communications insights, however, were not the only thing that happened for me. From this experience, through Rafe's roaring, I realized that whatever I did or didn't do I would be deeply criticized and often misunderstood by the people I was trying to work with. Whether or not I could "win" had nothing to do with anything. I am who I am, a White, overeducated, New England Puritan Yankee female. I mustn't expect to be understood, praised, or even effective. I have to follow my conscience, my opportunities, my experience wherever they lead, as faithful as I can be to my own inner vision.

Words Of Wisdom From Malcolm X

"What can a sincere White person do?

"When I say that here now, it makes me think about the little coed I told you about, the one who came up to me in the Nation of Islam's restaurant in Harlem, and I told her there was 'nothing' she could do. I regret that I told her that. I wish now I could tell her what I tell White people now when they present themselves as being sincere and ask me, one way or another, the same thing that she asked me.

"The first thing I tell them is that at least where my own particular Black Nationalist organization, the Organization of Afro-American Unity, is concerned, they can't *join* us. I have these very deep feelings that White people who want to join Black organizations are really just taking the escapist way to salve their consciences. By visibly hovering near us, they are 'proving' that they are 'with us.' But the hard truth is that this *isn't* helping to solve America's racist problem. The Negroes aren't the racists. Where the really sincere White people have got to do their 'proving' of themselves is not among the Black *victims*, but on the battle lines of where America's racism really *is*—and that's in their own home communities. Americans' racism is among their own fellow Whites. That's where the sincere Whites who really mean to accomplish something have got to work.

"... generally Whites' very presence subtly renders the Black organization automatically less effective. Even the best White members will slow down the Negroes' discovery of what they need to do and particularly of what they can do—for themselves, working by themselves, among their own kind, in their own communities . . . But anyway, know that every time that Whites join a Black organization, you watch, pretty soon the Blacks will be leaning on the Whites to support it, and before you know it, a Black may be up front with a title, but the Whites, because of their money, are the real controllers.

"I tell sincere White people, 'Work in conjunction with us—each of us working among our own kind.' Let sincere White individuals find all the other White people they can who feel as they do—and let them form their own all-White groups, to work trying to convert other White people who are thinking and acting so racist. Let sincere Whites go and teach nonviolence to White people.

"Working separately, the sincere White people and the sincere Black people actually will be working together. In our mutual sincerity, we might be able to show a road to the salvation of America's very soul. It can only be salvaged if human rights and dignity, in full, are extended to Black men [and women]. Only such real, meaningful actions as those which are sincerely motivated from a deep sense of humanism and moral responsibility can get at the basic causes that produce the racial explosions in America today."
—from *Autobiography of Malcolm X*, pp. 366-7

Let's think about this. Change "Negro" to any other minority group. How can "sincere" members of a "dominant" group most effectively work to shift a racist climate of their community? Does Malcolm X make sense? How would you respond to his comments?

12

Education

The goal of public education is to acculturate the young into the dominant American culture. Emphasis is on the heritage, systems, sciences, myths and goals of the United States. It is intended to send graduates out into the world to help build the United States as we wish it were.

What does this do for the many minority peoples whose heritage is disparaged and who, for many reasons, have never felt an accepted part of American society? "Acculturation" usually means the destruction or abandonment of their traditional values and lifeways, and they frequently feel excluded from the "American Dream."

Education: An Introduction

Though many wise and experienced educators are struggling with the challenges of our public school system, problems continue. Too familiar to list, these problems have put us in almost last place in national surveys of educational effectiveness, and they affect a whole range of economic and social conditions.

Those who can afford it are shunted off to our excellent private schools and go on to elite colleges from which they seldom return. That leaves the vast range of middle and lower income families resorting to the opportunities available. Their graduates are the future of Santa Fe and New Mexico.

It's a mixture. Some good schools, some failing. Some excellent teachers; some frustrated by the challenges, some who should never enter a classroom. Some programs popular, others merely endured. Some students eager, to the delight of their teachers, many merely indifferent. Some schools held to standards, others remain casual. Some open to improvements, others seem hopeless.

Of course, many students do well and go on to college or careers. Others need intense remedial work before they are ready for college courses. Others simply give up, drop out, make do.

It's said that programs that work well in other places consistently fail in New Mexico. After all, Santa Fe is "The City Different," New Mexico is "The Land of Enchantment." What else do we need? PLENTY, including education. But it has to be relevant, engaging, flexible, lifelong for all ages.

I wonder. Do the educational administrators, many from elsewhere, consider the complex intercultural dynamics at work here, as much as they can be discerned? They are certainly factors in all that we see and do.

The comments of the following *Voices* are by no means the whole story, far from it. But they offer insights worth considering as we struggle to improve the schools for us all.

Education: Voices

"History is boring. Who cares what happened long ago? What's it got to do with me? We live in the now and that's all that matters. I can't be bothered with all that old stuff. It's all lies, anyway."
—An Anglo high school student

❖❖❖

"We've got some history too. Why don't they teach it to us? It might be useful to know about our ancestors and what happened to them. It would help us understand what's happening to us now."
—A Hispanic high school student

❖❖❖

"Many of the students I work with at the Institute of American Indian Arts are urban Indians who have grown up far from their traditional homelands and people. They know a lot about poverty and discrimination. They are angry, lost and sad and don't know who or what they are as Indians. The first thing we have to teach them is how to understand and claim their own heritage, to learn what it means to be Indian. One of the ways I do this is by bringing in elders from many tribes who spend several weeks here, sharing their traditional wisdom with the students. What a difference it makes! They gain a sense of confidence and pride, they know what they stand for, and it shows in the way they walk, in the quality of their art."

—A teacher at IAIA

❖❖❖

"Our history teacher took us downtown last week where a museum docent gave us a tour. I've been to the Plaza many, many times but never really looked at what's there. The docent showed us monuments and markers and told us stories about the people and events they commemorate, all the way from the statue of Don Pedro de Peralta designing the town to the Indians under the portal at the Governors' Palace. Good things, not-so-good things, my hometown came alive for me in a new way and I want to learn more. And I've changed my mind about the Civil War obelisk in the middle of the plaza. Now that I see what it means, I don't want it moved away."

—Hispanic student

❖❖❖

"These kids are lost! They have no contact with their families or their communities. They feel that nobody understands them or cares about them. They yearn to belong. They gather in tribes, in gangs, in clusters, seeking love and support and surrogate families. But without roots, they drift around aimlessly, without focus, direction or hope. There are masses of them, searching. They are the REAL challenge for our community, for our future. We do what we can, but we are so few and they are so many, and the need is so great. Our multicultural community, in all its dimensions, has work to do."

—A youth worker

❖❖❖

"Sure, my kids are dropouts. I don't want the school system to damage them as much as it damaged me. I was forbidden to speak, or to learn the language of my grandparents and punished if I spoke Spanish with my friends

All I remember the books taught us about our heritage was that the Spaniards were cruel to the Indians and that the Americans "rescued" us when they took our land away from Mexico. Most of the teachers didn't seem to know more about us than that. They often treated us Hispanic kids as if we were dumb, and maybe we were. There were hints we "wouldn't make it," whatever that meant. Some teachers were caring and tried to help us, but there was a lot of misunderstanding and sometimes open racism. I learned to feel bad about myself and my heritage and inferior to the White people. I've struggled for years to overcome that feeling. I don't want my kids to go through all that. Has anything changed?"

—A Hispanic parent

❖❖❖

"The education professor was speaking to our class of graduate students. She wanted to know why, in our opinion, so many Hispanic students do so badly in school and so often drop out. One of our classmates, a Hispanic woman more outspoken than most, startled us by asserting that they are a conquered people. If they do well in school they're cooperating with their oppressors to their great sorrow. They can't admit their defeat and destruction of their culture. They won't betray their people and become "Americans." This really started the discussion flowing. We wondered what, if anything, we as teachers can do about it."

—A participant

❖❖❖

"We're trying. We're teaching a lot more about cultural heritages in our school. We have Intercultural days, Who Are You sessions, family histories, food tastings, fashion shows. But you know. Nobody seems to care."

—Frustrated teacher

❖❖❖

"What does it <u>do</u> to a person when the schoolteachers beat him or her for speaking their own language? What does it do when nothing positive is taught about his heritage? What does it do when official policies try to eradicate his culture, breaking the links with family and all that has gone before?

What does it do when the history of the United States is taught with no positive mention of the Indian and Hispanic cultures? What does it do to people who are "educated" into the mainstream yet find nothing but prejudice and rejection when seeking employment and a future in this same mainstream? What does it do when your self-confidence and any positive self-image are disparaged and erased by the surrounding media? Sure, they are trying to turn us into productive Americans, even though they destroy us in the process. Generations of New Mexicans are hurting, bitter, lost. I'm lucky, I seem to be doing OK. But inside . . . you don't want to see."

—A creative Hispanic woman educator

❖❖❖

"In my seventh grade class an Indian girl from Taos appeared yesterday. She seemed shy and scared. I tried to make her feel welcome and appreciated. I looked at her, spoke to her, asked her questions in my most friendly manner. New students in my classes have always responded well to my efforts. But this girl didn't. She shut down. She wouldn't look at me. She spoke, if at all, in a barely audible monotone. Then she disappeared and never came back. What did I do wrong? How can I get her back? I've never had this kind of a problem before. What should I do?"

—A young teacher new to New Mexico

❖❖❖

"Those Mexican kids in that fifth grade classroom are learning English but they are so far behind the class work that they can't keep up with the others. The poor teacher is struggling, her Spanish is poor, and the kids are falling through the cracks. The principal doesn't know what to do about it, so she has sent the kids down to the kindergarten rooms to help the teachers there. Aren't there better ways to deal with situations like this?"

—A classroom volunteer

❖❖❖

"Naw. School doesn't have anything to do with me. What's the point? It's boring. The teachers don't know how to talk with us. The work they assign is stupid. I ditch as often as I can and will soon drop out completely. I can make good money, enough for—substances. My folks don't care. Why should I bother?"

—Hispanic kid smoking in an arroyo

❖❖❖

"What's the matter with those school administrators? New buildings, fancy facilities, innovative programs are only window dressing, like rearranging chairs on the Titanic. They're not going to change the dropout situation. They have to figure out how to motivate the students, to persuade them that education is worth the effort, that there's a future for them. That's a job for the whole community, not just the schools."

—High school senior

❖❖❖

"Why did I drop out? I had better things to do with my time. I was starting my own business, learning what I needed to know on the job and reading a lot about things that interest me. School was too slow. I often knew more than the teachers, and was forced into irrelevant courses, wasting my time. College? Why bother? I can learn more from life."

—A dropout

❖❖❖

"The schools are excellent here, the private ones, that is. My son got a good, rounded education and is now at Harvard. My daughter is enjoying the academic challenges and doing well. My youngest is waiting eagerly for the inspiring teachers he has heard about. Too bad the educational level of the public schools is so bad—but we have to look after our own."

—Anglo parent

13

Conflict

$\mathcal{B}$elow the surface of our lively, creative, appealing community there are hurting, confused and angry individuals of many backgrounds. Some are suffering from cultural tensions or cultural damage. Others are irate at the abuses inflicted on the community and its people by those in authority. Still others are struggling against ignorance, indifference and resistance to change, struggles that may benefit everybody.

How we handle conflict is crucial. It can mean pathways to hope or escalating resentment, solutions to problem areas or frustration and loss.

Conflict Here And Now

$\mathcal{C}$onflict is inevitable in multicultural communities like ours. Change is happening fast. Change brings pain as well as opportunity. Change brings stresses, strains, conflict. Change challenges all of us, particularly when we move out of our "comfort zone," or some outside factor intrudes.

Conflicts may be as personal as with the sour neighbor whose dog pees all over your flowers. Or as apparently reprehensible as the actions of the local police. Or as broad as resistance to the multinational corporations exploiting sparse regional resources for their own profit. They may be anything in between.

People often may—or may not—feel they have to get involved in one way or another. Some are "Ain't it awful" bystanders who lament but do little. Others are "We HAVE to DO something" activists who lend their energies to the cause. Some are pretty indifferent, blissfully unaware of the tensions swirling around them. Others seize the opportunity to reach out and engage.

Most of us, I think, respond in different ways to different situations, at different times and places.

Conflicts come in many styles and degrees of intensity. Let's look at some of them.

Sources Of Conflict

National/International Issues. Though these originate elsewhere, their vibrations resonate everywhere, setting neighbors into yelling matches, stony silences, or at least tense discussions. Foreign relations, abortion, taxes, global warming, exploitation of the environment, creationism, immigration, and themes like these can escalate conflicts among friends, bring conversations to a halt, cut off communications. *"That woman believes in gay marriage and is always bragging about her female spouse—I can't talk with her any* more." or *"That man is so proud of his son in the military, calls him his hero even though he murdered Iraq civilians in their beds—it's too much!"* Conflicting values on display. Can we agree to disagree?

Community Issues bring conflicts closer to home. Police actions, educational policies, juvenile justice, job access, parking problems, personal safety, curfews, almost every area where racism, discrimination, prejudice might possibly play a part, has options for conflict. Sometimes they can be settled amicably, sometimes not. Sometimes community pressure can force resolution, and sometimes, if ignored, the conflict evaporates by itself.

Personal Conflicts involve individuals. The neighbor whose dogs bark all night; the teacher who flunked your son, the druggie who infected your daughter; the cop who hassled your Mexican friend; the employer who fired you for no reason . . . such situations arise every day. Sometimes mediation or lawsuits or personal visits can soothe the conflicts, but sometimes conflicts just fester.

Family Conflict is particularly tragic. Changing values can set generations against each other. Abuse of drugs and alcohol can lead to violence. Relationships can shift from caring to conflict, sometimes with beatings that lead to death. The young often run away, escaping from intolerable pressures. Psychological abuse can mark victims for years. Small conflicts are normal, a process in growth, and can lead to new insights, but when they escalate they can shatter the family structure. Sometimes the law and social services have to intervene, and sometimes, with time, relationships heal.

Philosophical Conflict can be just a devastating as the physical kind. You've seen politicians battling over scarce funds and competing visions for the future. Academics and scientists fighting for the validity of their research. Religious fanatics debating (!) the characteristics of their god, and they can get brutal! Spouses screaming about their contrasting styles of childrearing. And even though such conflicts seem abstract, the after effects can ruin lives.

Internal Conflict occurs when individuals struggle within themselves over identity, actions and relationships. "Who will be hurt if I come out as gay?" " Should I leave next month for the distant job offered, even though it will crush my family?" "Will he acknowledge the new baby or should I ditch the guy?" "How does the relationship with my pueblo limit my future?" Internal conflicts like these can tear apart the fabric of one's being. They must be resolved, with or without help.

Finally, Denial. Insisting that "everything is fine" even though it isn't. Papering over conflicts, pretending they don't exist. I think we all go through phases of denial about certain things. We can't really deal with them until we're ready to take them out and look at them. Sometimes they dissolve when circumstances change; sometimes they just fade away on their own. Sometimes they fester for years. A caring friend can often help just by being there with a listening ear and new perspectives.

Conflict And Us

Most of us, I think, don't handle conflict very well. At least I know I don't. When someone challenges a cherished assumption, or attacks the way I live my life, or scorns my actions and beliefs, or tears down what I've been trying to build up, or denigrates my person, I tend to react badly.

Sometimes I counter attack, or storm away in a fury. Or scream irrelevancies. Or retreat to lick my wounds.

It's not until the next day when I can calm down and consider the challenge rationally that I realize, maybe there's some truth in the unwelcome perspective. Maybe there isn't. How should I respond? In this instance, what do I stand up for? Or what do I need to reconsider? Where do I draw the line?

Of course, it works the other way, too. Appalled at a particular situation or attitude, we can challenge other people in turn. Our attacks can be as vicious as our opponents', scorning the person as well as the position.

When we are involved in the heat of the moment, and afterwards, what can we do?

Do you remember the signs by the old railroad crossings? Maybe we can: STOP, LOOK and LISTEN

Stop everything. Take a deep breath. A moment's break can reduce tension. Eat a cookie. Drink some tea. Offer something to your opponent. Remember he/she is a person worthy of respect, not merely a position we disagree with.

Look. Where are we? With whom? What's the context? Who else is involved? Why? What's the desired outcome? What's the best way to proceed? How are we behaving in this situation?

Listen. What's actually being said or promoted versus what we think is being said? Can we squash tendencies to yell, blame, accuse? Are we all sticking to the point or running off in irrelevancies and past hassles? What are we ourselves saying, and how?

Of course, we want to win. But what does winning mean in this situation? Do we want to completely destroy our opponents and send them away in disgrace with their tails between their legs? Do we simply want to be acknowledged and heard? Do we want our ideas to prevail, to be accepted, to be acted upon? Do we want to develop dialogue about complex problems in hopes of resolving them? Do we want to turn our opponents into partners with both perspectives contributing to the whole? Do we want attitudes and actions to change?

We don't have to agree. We probably won't. But we can be polite about it. Disagreement can be creative, adversaries can become allies. The larger issues can absorb smaller ones, core values unite peripherals. Conflict can be a positive tool for positive change. It can sharpen and strengthen our positions, and warn us when they are foolish or inadequate.

Please, somebody, remind me of these things when I'm under attack.

As Outsiders, How Can We Help In Conflict Situations?

Most of the time we can't. We need to know when to back off, to stay out of such situations. We seldom understand all the key issues involved, whether within or across cultures. Outside "meddlers" can make a bad situation worse, and often do. Yet outsiders, from whatever background, can make a positive difference.

What do we have to offer? Probably more than we realize. A listening ear, a caring presence. A general understanding of the New Mexican heritage. Wide perspectives that may be relevant. A sense of the values that steer our course. Lifelong experience with living. Contacts, resources and networks possibly pertinent. Respect for the people we are with. And ourselves.

Perhaps a caring, non-judgmental listening as we try to comprehend the context and emotions as well as the words may be the best gift we can offer. Careful questioning can break down the general amorphous wrath into smaller components that can be dealt with individually. Listening does not imply agreement: on the contrary, sometimes it reveals contentious issues that need attention as part of the larger whole. Yet simply being "heard" often leads to healing and new approaches to dealing with the dilemma under consideration.

Solitude, isolation and stress can inhibit clear thinking about a conflict. We outsiders may have a broader outlook than the struggling local. We may have dealt with similar situations before, or know about some pertinent resources, organizations or individuals. Sources of help, forgotten or unrecognized, may be close at hand. We outsiders can point the way toward them as appropriate.

Remember, we are outsiders and the conflict is not ours to solve. Let those involved initiate the action. We need to eliminate he words "should" and "ought" in telling others what to do. We can describe how similar challenges were handled elsewhere, we can lay out some possible options, and we can let the affected folks take over the next steps. We must respect their decisions even when we think they are wrong. We can help celebrate success when it happens.

Yes. We can help where we can. But we have to be careful not to be drawn into other people's conflicts any more than is comfortable for us. It's okay to say "No, not now. Sorry. Maybe later." We do have our own lives to live, even while caring about larger conflicts and the people who struggle with them successfully—or not.

In Conflict Situations We Can:

Listen. Listen to all sides with courtesy and respect. Listen to the people involved, to the problems and the possibilities. Listen to more than the words: to the context, the background, the values, the personal issues. Listening does not necessarily mean agreement, though it can open the way for creative dialogue. "Being heard" is half the battle. Sometimes listening is the best gift we can offer hurting individuals, and our attention, voiced or not, can heal distress and set a new course.

Think Specific. A generalized emotional outpouring of "Ain't it awful" can be pretty overwhelming. Break it up into smaller segments. Are there key issues around which the others revolve? Are some more easily approached than others? Movement on a small piece of the problem provides a sense of progress that can animate the whole process.

Research. Who is doing what about the particular problem under discussion? In every area there are some good folks or organizations working creatively with ideas, experience and contacts. Some of them might be pertinent to the current situation. Too often we feel alone as we struggle to define the issues and choose a course of action, or reaction. Not so.

Network. Go ahead and connect with appropriate resources to help deal with the roots of the conflict. Nobody has all the answers or all the energy to "solve" problems, but everybody has insights that may help. When we can talk about our conflicts, our perspectives broaden and we can think about them in different ways.

Refresh. Take a break. Do something besides talking and fretting and stewing about the problem. Take a walk. Paint a picture. Plant some flowers. Go to a movie. Eat some ice cream. When we return to the subject, maybe new energy and insights will appear.

Communicate. When other people realize what is going on, we may be surprised at the support and encouragement they can provide. Or alternatively, correctives that can save us from embarrassment or disaster.

Persist. Nothing happens overnight. Problems that have developed over years will take time to resolve. Misunderstandings and frustrations are normal aspects of the process. When we fall on our faces, we need to get up and try again, though this is often hard to do. When people laugh at us—or with us—we can laugh, too, and cry when we need to. Don't give up, let time help.

Compromise when we can; Resist when we can't. What kind of outcome do we want? How do we define "success" in this situation? How much are we willing to compromise? How deeply have we listened and understood all pertinent points of view? What are the values involved? What are the chances of appropriate action?

Disagree? Sometimes we may be appalled at what we hear. It may seem crazy, or ignorant, or dangerous, or just plain evil. Values can clash, experience can limit or expand reactions, environment may isolate from alternative realities. How we respond depends on the situation. It could be anything from persuasion, to condemnation, to calling in the authorities. Or when the cultural gulf is too wide, we may simply have to leave it alone.

And Celebrate. Applaud every success along the way. As we mark progress step by step, the conflicts change their tone. When victims become activists, when we can meet our adversaries with calm dialogue, smiles and a party, we'll know that we have all won.

14

Vistas

$\mathcal{E}$ach of these situations was actually witnessed by me or reported by a reliable informer. How would you respond in each case?

$\mathcal{A}$ community group in Santa Fe has been trying to gather a citizens' council to consider action on a particular concern and related programs. The leaders are caring Anglos who think they are well integrated into the community. The first meeting brought out about twenty people, eight of them Hispanic, the rest of them Anglo. At the second meeting there were only two Hispanics in attendance. By the third meeting, there were none at all.

"What have we done wrong?" lamented the organizers. "This is a program for all of us. We need Hispanic input and participation, but they don't seem to care! They don't come to meetings! Why not? What can we do to attract and keep them?"

❖ ❖ ❖

I was invited to talk with a group of Land Grant activists in Tierra Amarilla. The politics of the area are fragmented with feuding factions, the passions run high, and threats of violence are always present. Yet, I felt that the person who has invited me was trying to bring healing, hope and some coordination to a chaotic situation. I admired her courage, and I appreciated her confidence that I might have something useful to offer.

Two days before the event, I received a phone call from one of the rival leaders up there. He warned me not to participate, that the workshop leader "is not from here and therefore suspect," that the whole community would boycott the event. "Be careful, something might happen to you . . ." The implied threat was not very veiled.

It's a two-hour trip from Santa Fe. I felt my time was valuable and could be used profitably for other things. My little red car was distinctive, and on the long, lonely road hasslers could easily run me into a ditch or cause trouble of some kind. My spouse was scared for me, but would not accompany me. Participation would mean a major effort with no guaranteed results. I learned that my friend had received several death threats but was not deterred.

This was my dilemma: what should I do at this point? (you say!)

❖❖❖

A newcomer to New Mexico remarked, appalled, "What's this crazy idea I've heard about, you New Mexicans sending a statue of a rebel (Popé) to Washington? Can't you come up with somebody more appropriate for the National Hall of Statues?"

❖❖❖

A handsome young Indian studying here in Santa Fe looked troubled. I asked him what was bothering him. "I'm living with a White girl. She wants me to get a job, to bring in some money for household expenses. But I can't do that!" he told me. "I'm a Sioux, a warrior. Warriors don't work. We don't pay the bills. That's women's work."

❖❖❖

A visiting family has just returned from a day in one of the mountain villages. Father, mother and two kids all seem delighted with the experience. The mother glowed,

It was wonderful. A weaver invited us into his shop and showed us the whole process from sheep to sale and the fine old tools he uses and the loom his grandfather had made, and he set the kids up to try their hand at weaving. We told him about the crafts we do at home—I make quilts and my husband builds ship models—and we talked about our lives. He took us into his house where his wife taught my daughter to make empanaditas and they fed us a delicious lunch. Then they left the shop to an assistant and drove us up into the hills to show us the dye and medicinal plants they use. . . . They wouldn't accept any money except for the rug we bought. They were so warm and friendly! How can we ever repay them?

Their Santa Fe hosts, who had not gone along, were appalled. "How could you?" they protested. "Business is OK, and to visit the shop. But their home? Such people are dirty and ignorant and superstitious, and were probably out to exploit you in some way. You ate there? You'll probably get sick. We've got to keep some distance if we want their respect!" (Could this happen in Santa Fe?)

❖ ❖ ❖

A pretty young Hispanic girl was tending the information desk. A visitor, a huge, burly Texan strode up to her. Leaning over her, he shoved his face a few inches from hers, and he ROARED, "Aren't you ashamed for what your ancestors did to the Indians? How can you live with yourself?" He puffed up his chest and strode away, as proud as if he had won a war.

The poor girl was in shock. The attack was so brutal and unexpected. Her grandmother was a Pueblo Indian, and she had always been proud of her mixed heritage. She dissolved in tears and ran out, sobbing.

I had seen this episode but I was too astonished to react right away. I didn't know whether to go after the Texan who by now had disappeared, or to go comfort the girl who had also disappeared. Nobody else seemed to have noticed the incident. I've been seething ever since.

❖ ❖ ❖

A friend believed she had really goofed. At Santa Clara's Puye Cliffs, she was trying to help a visiting eleven-year-old visualize the people who might have lived there long ago. In the process, they were examining bits of debris and small fragments of broken pottery along the trail. After countless admonitions of "Don't touch," "Put it back," she finally conceded that the girl could take a couple of little pieces to show her mother waiting in the parking lot below. Appreciation for the skills of the ancient ones had overridden respect for the living ones.

An observant ranger, a huge, angry Indian who had been watching them through binoculars confronted the two as they moved down the trail. Appropriately, he gave them holy hell. Since they had ignored the posted prohibitions about picking up or removing objects, he told them to leave the area immediately. Penalties were usually much tougher, large fines or jail, he told them.

The young visitor was in tears. My friend felt totally chagrined because she normally tries so hard to be culturally sensitive and responsible. Over the next weeks, she reported that the incident, instead of fading away, continued to rankle in her conscience. What should she do? How serious was her blunder? How can she make things right?

❖❖❖

An Indian, a middle-aged professional working in a federal job serving his people (very well, from all accounts), was astonishingly candid with us, a small group of *Vecinos* and me, an Anglo he barely knew. He explained that he grew up in a local pueblo. He went away to get an education and entered a whole new world. He earned two masters degrees and had almost completed his doctorate. He had traveled all over the world, owned land and condos in many places across the country. He had thoroughly enjoyed a yuppie lifestyle, was happy with its openness, stimulus and variety, and with the many diverse friends it had brought him.

Since his assignment to Santa Fe, he had returned to his pueblo, renewed contact with his family, friends and heritage. He joined the dances, advised the elders, participated in Pueblo affairs however he could.

But soon, he would be ready for early retirement. He was convinced that the Pueblo elders, who appreciated his skills and experience, were watching him carefully and would probably ask him to become part of the Pueblo council, even perhaps Governor, to spend the rest of his life helping his people. "A fate worse than death," he described. "It is such a dirty, backward, limited community, and once you get into leadership roles there is no way out." He couldn't give up his personal professional freedom to "rot" in the pueblo, yet he could not be the first Indian ever to refuse to serve when asked by the council. He didn't know what to do or how to resolve the dilemma.

❖❖❖

I was in charge of meetings, each with a particular task to accomplish. Most people present were usually Anglos with a smattering of Indians or

Hispanics. Though I always carefully laid out the agenda ahead of time, soon one of the Hispanics (or Indians) stood up with a concern reflecting deep-level pain and went on and on about it. I couldn't quite see how this related to the theme of the meeting, but I did not want to shut off this person's story. Yet some of the others present were acting puzzled and restless and I felt obligated to continue with the task at hand. The speaker needed attention and I wanted to give it, but so did the Anglo participants. How to proceed was often a dilemma.

❖❖❖

The Forest Ranger was hot and bothered. He looked disheveled, exhausted and discouraged. He accepted the cold Coke I offered him and slumped down on a nearby bench. "Those Hispanic guys from that village, they're stubborn, they're stupid, they can't—or won't—understand."

"What's the problem?" I asked, sitting down beside him.

"They care more about their darned cows than the environment," he grumbled. "There's no way the land can support all the animals they insist it's their 'traditional right' to bring in to the forest for the summer. There's too many, in spite of attempts to limit the numbers, and they always manage to sneak some more in. Every time we put up a temporary fence to let an area recover, they tear it down. The riverbanks are all eroded, waterholes polluted, grazing land destroyed, brush and small stuff inviting fires. We're trying to restore and preserve the forest for them and their families, but to them we of the Forest Service are the hated *floresta,* the enemy. They seem to think we want to destroy their lifestyle, when we want to save it. But they won't listen, and soon their forest land will be worthless. What can we say or do? Can you help?

Can you? Any ideas?

❖❖❖

"We came for our *piñones*," the smiling woman announced. I couldn't figure out if she was Hispanic or Pueblo, as several other folks and kids clustered around her.

The man on the other side of the high wire fence merely growled, "Go away!" I had come to see him on some business, and I was a bit dismayed at his abrupt manner.

"Please, señor. Let us in. Those *piñon* trees are ours. We've collected nuts from those trees for generations, the time of our fathers and grandfathers. We'll just pick the *piñones* and then go away. We won't bother you."

"Scram. This is private property now. I paid good money for it and you are not welcome here."

"But señor, you don't need the *piñones*. We do and the land has been part of our family . . ."

He interrupted with a shrill whistle that brought two big dogs running, snarling and threatening the folks on the other side of the fence. "Get out before I call the cops," he roared.

I was scared.

"Git!" he hollered, and the disappointed people turned away, kids crying. He grabbed my arm and pulled me toward the house. "We've got business," he reminded. "Those dirty people don't count."

I waved helplessly at the woman who scowled at me. I was seething with fury. Smoke must have been pouring out of my ears. What could I say to this man that might make a difference?

How might you have handled this situation?

❖ ❖ ❖

One day I was talking with a developer who was planning a huge new residential complex in our dry, semi-desert region. "Where do you expect to find enough water for all the people in this project?" I asked.

He smiled and assured me, "No problem. All we have to do it to eliminate all those little farms along the Rio Grande and its tributaries. Agriculture is a totally wasteful use of water. Get rid of the farms and we'll have plenty of water for all the people we want to house."

I was appalled. Was he serious? (He was!) "What about the farmers whose families have lived and worked the land for generations?"

"Don't worry about them," he insisted. "They'll adapt. They'll be OK. They'll move somewhere else." He towered over me and patted me on the head. "Don't worry, little lady. Without those farms there'll be more than enough water to drink."

(This really happened. No, I didn't slug him. He was too big.)

❖ ❖ ❖

Another day a *Vecinos* group was visiting a small farm in one of the up-country villages, welcomed by our venerable hostess. Somebody knocked softly at the door. A few words and our hostess grabbed the rifle behind the door and disappeared. We wondered what was going on.

She returned a few minutes later without the gun. A government water inspector was in the neighborhood, she explained. "We don't like government people nosing around here, especially inspectors. If he messes up our acequias—that's our water ditches—he can disrupt irrigation of our fields for months. If he thinks we're abusing our allotment, he can take us to court, a horrible nuisance. Our acequia system is so well balanced and maintained that one interfering nincompoop could disrupt it severely. We don't want him here."

"What did you do? Did you shoot him?" one of our number inquired.

She laughed. "Oh no, that wasn't necessary—this time. All I have to do is to set my grandson on the head gate, which controls the water flow, with a rifle in his hands and a fierce look on his face. He's sixteen and usually doesn't look fierce at all. That's all. The inspector takes one look, gets scared, and quietly goes away. We've had no trouble with inspectors for years."

❖ ❖ ❖

Off Roaders now had full use of the mesa top, in spite of government's arrangements protecting the ranchers who grazed their cattle in the area. One of the Hispanic ranchers I often talked with complained bitterly, his usually friendly face twisted in anger.

"Those guys (he used a stronger word) with their four-wheelers and trucks are destroying the land. They carve illegal ruts they call roads across the landscape, they cut fences, they scare the cattle and scatter them, they turn our stock tanks into mud pits and tear down our windmills, they race around like crazy, they build bonfires, and they even occasionally kill a cow for a barbecue. When we protest, they threaten us with guns and clubs. The rangers pay no attention. But the worst thing is that we—ranchers, roaders and government officials—came together for months to work out a new agreement for use of the land that was fair to all of us, and then the government lady called us Hispanics some bad names and ignored us in favor of the rich White roaders who have no responsibility or oversight and can do whatever they want. We local Hispanics just don't count, and that hurts."

This was the subject of several newspaper articles in 2012.

15

What Can We Do Now?

Challenges fester wherever people of one culture coexist with people of others.

Sometimes the resulting stresses are obvious, sometimes simmering beneath the surface, sometimes violent, and sometimes are resolved in ways that satisfy all parties.

Sometimes, the cultural gulfs are enormous chasms, separated by value systems abhorrent to both.

Often, they are international as well as intercultural, with puzzled diplomats, business promoters, and development workers struggling to find common ground.

Basic issues can be divisive: role of women, religious influence, focus of education, access to food and housing, dignity of individuals, meaning of freedom, immigration status, use of violence.

"Culture" can include many subsets: gender, countercultures, political systems, employment patterns, community traditions.

Sometimes, cultural stresses and gaps can be resolved, or at least mitigated, when people care to listen and then take appropriate action. And sometimes not.

We live in an era of increasing polarization, of uncivil discourse, of conformity, of exploitation of the environment, of abuse of power, of electronic gadgets, of ethnocentrism and violence toward others, of disregard for human dignity, of alarming headlines—enough to frighten us into helpless passivity.

But we also live in an era in which many, many, many people are struggling creatively to heal the wounds, to preserve traditions, to restore dignity, to cross the gaps, to struggle with the challenges, to bring people together. . . . But it's hard to hear them over the noise of the negatives.

Are You One Of These?

I call them "Cultural Interpreters"—but there ought to be a jazzier name.

They are people of every background who are aware and who care. You can be Anglo, Indian, Hispanic, Mexican, Navajo, something else, or none of the above. You can be wealthy—or limited—in material goods, or in experience, in education, in wisdom, in resources, in the business of living.

Can you see beyond the length of your nose? Can you listen? Do you understand your own heritage and values—more or less? Are you open to alternative perspectives and various ideas without losing your own? Are you aware of the resources available in your community? Can you relax and enjoy connections with others different from yourself?

Cultural interpreters are people who:

Understand and respect cultural diversity and who are working in many ways to preserve and affirm the values and strengths of different traditions.

Struggle with the complexities of cultures in collision, as rapid social and community changes threaten the values of traditional lifeways.

Recognize the contributions that each culture offers to the larger community, and fight against easy stereotypes, subtle racism, injustice,

Offer practical help however they can for resolving problems, building relationships, and affirming the value and humanity of each person.

Don't have all the answers but are stumbling along, doing the best they can, learning and growing, and enjoying the process.

They may be artists, educators, parents, writers, senior citizens, community workers, youth leaders, government officials, pastors, farmers, philosophers, business owners, teachers, tour guides, legislators, councilors, doctors, bums, church members. In every profession occasional situations emerge where a person, a cultural interpreter, can make a difference. Few of us can relate to the whole spectrum of intercultural opportunities, but within the framework of our lives we have much to offer.

Are you one of these?

Some Suggestions For Things We Can Do Now:

FIRST:

We can recognize that our intercultural situation needs attention. So-called ethnic tensions are simmering beneath the surface, the "cultural gaps" widening. Each of us, whatever our heritage, education, income or length of time in New Mexico, can do something about them. The problems that face our community—education, jobs, gangs, justice, water, abuse, development, you name it—affect all of us and can be resolved only if we are cross-cultural allies rather than antagonists.

Intercultural relationships can be as complicated as an active, lifetime commitment, or as simple as the first friendly smile or handshake. In between, lie a vast variety of opportunities for enlightenment, enrichment and action. Each step along the way moves us a little farther along in the process of building multicultural comfort and community.

It's as much attitude as action.

SECOND:

We can reach out to make personal contacts across the cultures. For some of this it is hard to do. We're afraid of being rebuffed, misunderstood, exploited somehow—and sometimes these things do happen. Don't be surprised if the other person has the same fears about you. But when we make the effort and connect with neighbors, work, community and organization associates, we often find a warm and open response that leads to unexpected friendship.

Sometimes a simple invitation for coffee and conversation, or a shared laugh at some silly antic, or presence at a neighborhood event, or indignation about political shenanigans can start the process. Sharing food often leads to other sharing: life stories, ideas, experiences, community concerns. Contacts begun at a ballgame, a Pueblo feast day, a company picnic, a neighborhood meeting, a chance encounter at the Plaza, can ripen into a valued relationship. People-to-people communicating and relating across the cultures can create a movement of healing and bridging the cultural gaps that so often separate us.

THIRD:

We can replace cultural stereotypes with personal stories. Stereotypes are inevitable as we try to make sense out of our cross-cultural expectations and experiences. They can be positive or negative, but they often blind us to the incredible diversity of individuals within each cultural group.

Each of us has a story that sets us apart as the individuals we are. If we can learn to listen to each other on many different levels, then the experiences, struggles, and aspirations begin to emerge. The stories of others encourage us to look more deeply into our own heritage. Such sharing can pull us together.

FOURTH:

We need to respect the dignity of each person, though their viewpoints may be different from ours. When we don't understand, we need to listen more carefully. When we are not understood, we need to rephrase what we are trying to say. We can disagree without denying the integrity of the individual and the validity of their experience. We can affirm a caring spirit even as we try to work through confusions and possible conflicts. Sometimes, we have to agree to disagree while seeking areas of agreement.

FIFTH:

We all need to learn more about the people of the area, and also about our own heritage. Libraries are filled with helpful and fascinating books; videos and DVDs abound. Museum exhibits, lectures, presentations, and newspaper articles can extend our understanding. Occasional workshops can help us deal with communications and conflict resolution. Language study can illuminate the thought patterns of other cultures and—hopefully—provide deeper appreciation of our neighbors who "live in two worlds."

But theoretical learning should always be balanced with people, contacts, and consideration of issues affecting their lives—and vice versa. For one without the other is like trying to walk with only one foot.

SIXTH:

We are already involved, whether we realize it or not. Casual contacts can lead to action, whether as simple as writing the newspaper, or as ongoing as tutoring in a school, or participating in an awareness march, or sitting through long council meetings. Or the action leading to personal connections could be the other way around. Sometimes, our particular skills turn out to be useful, or our personal connections fill a need, or we can find essential resources to apply to a situation.

All these things are intertwined. Personal friendships can dissolve stereotypes. Relationships without commitment ring hollow. Action without information can backfire. Learning without involvement changes little. Books without personal contacts are sterile. We can start at any point along the way and expand from there in ever-widening circles. We must recognize that the process takes time for generations of misunderstanding and mistrust, often for very good reasons, do not change overnight. And the incredible "busyness" of our life in Santa Fe often overwhelms us.

But the important thing is to begin.

SEVENTH:

And we can lighten up.

What Else Can We Do? And How?

We can RELAX. Sit back. Put our feet up. Sip our drinks, whatever they may be. Watch and enjoy the passing parade. The human interest, the drama, the conflicts and creativity, the conversations and cheerful relationships that can keep us, of whatever heritage, interested for hours.

We can FORGET ABOUT EVERYTHING written in this book. What's useful will resurface when needed. Remember, we are involved with people, not abstract cultures, though people and their cultures are intertwined.

We can REACH OUT with a smile and an outstretched hand. We can look AT people, not through them; we can see them as the individuals they are. They may be more afraid of us than we are of them. So let's take the first step when appropriate. There are many kinds of people all around us: look, smile and relate. A simple "hello" can do wonders.

Where do we MEET PEOPLE? Wherever we are. Where we live, where we work and play and spend our time. Where we meet and eat and shop and study. Though some areas of our community are effectively segregated by money or custom, most are not, and interactions are possible. If someone doesn't want to talk, don't feel rejected. If someone is rude, we don't need to respond in kind. If someone is occupied, respect the privacy. But if someone has a few moments and a connection is made, rejoice!

We DON'T HAVE TO "LIKE" EVERYBODY. Some people are congenial, some are not. Some are totally uninterested or hostile, or dealing with un-resolved angers. Some may want to load us with "guilt trips" about ancient abuses: don't let them. Or they may want to exploit us somehow: be cautious. Even when someone's values, attitudes and actions clash violently with ours, we still may find common ground—and discover a treasure.

Occasionally, conversations will bring up PROBLEMS. Usually, listening is the best help we can give. We may know of community resources to suggest or have skills pertinent to the problem. Be careful not to get more involved than is comfortable, nor to promise more than you can deliver. And it's okay to SAY, NO, I don't want to get involved. If the problem is life threatening, call the authorities, don't try to handle it.

Above all, ENJOY THE PROCESS. It can be fascinating, delightful, enlightening, rewarding, enriching. And when we can make a difference, even a tiny one, we can celebrate.

16

Appendix

*T*hese pertinent items didn't seem to fit anywhere else, so here they are.

Alejandro's Plea:

"*W*hen you pass people in the street, look at them and relate."

This is the urgent request of Alejandro, whose dark eyes flash and whose cropped hair bristles with the intensity of his plea.

Alejandro was raised in Santa Cruz, educated at St. John's College in Santa Fe, and at schools in the east, where he earned degrees in Fine Arts and in Arts Education. His travels and varied cross-cultural experiences have made him a creative, multifaceted educator, especially in relation to his Hispanic heritage. As [then] Director of *Hispanosphere Intercultural Services,* he has provided many different presentations in bilingual, arts, and multicultural education.

Alejandro talks of the changes he has seen in recent years in our community and of his fears that Santa Fe may become "just another Anglo town" and he reminds us:

> "New people are pouring in from everywhere. They don't know the traditions, their rhythm is different, their relationships with others tend to be quick, cold, impersonal. Our own people are forgetting and finding it harder than ever to relate to people from different backgrounds. The city is becoming a cold, impersonal place where people seldom "see" each other, especially those of other cultural groups. Or they dismiss each other with stereotypes that often have little relationship to the complex humanity of individuals."

Even while lamenting, Alejandro urges action:

"It doesn't take much. Just notice the people around you. Don't worry if they look different, it their skin is darker or lighter than yours, if their clothes are simpler or fancier, if they talk different languages. Look at them and see them as individuals. Give them a smile, a nod, a hello. They may not know how to respond, but give them a chance. Even simple things like these can make a big difference about the way people feel about each other."

One of the gifts the Hispanic culture can offer to the rest of us, according to Alejandro, is a sense of connectedness to other people:

"My mother taught us always to be aware of the people around us, of who they are, of how they feel, of how to relate to them, to treasure their differences and the things they can share with us. Now, we see many people rushing around, intent on their own business with little time for human contacts. But even as Santa Fe grows, we can regain, and retain, the sense of a warm, people-oriented community—if we want to."

No, we can't bring back the old Santa Fe, he agrees. But maybe, by simply greeting each other across the cultures, we can recover some of its treasured spirit.
"Let's try it," he urges. "It's the least we can do. Let's see what happens."

❖ ❖ ❖

Here are comments from Roberto Chene of the Southwest Center for Cross-Cultural Relationships, at a *Vecinos* workshop, which reflected things he had often said. He occasionally served as an advisor and participant at many *Vecinos* functions. His main points:

No one "knows" how to create true multicultural community here in New Mexico, it has never been done. As a new "learning field," we're constantly experimenting, exploring, trying out ways that may, or may not, work out.

Educational systems, media, and mainstream expectations teach assimilation into the dominant culture, with little emphasis on intercultural respect, reconciliation, or bridging. This needs to change.

Intercultural collaboration is about relationships, not "studies" or "projects." Developing relationships, trust, connectedness, and community across the cultural lines takes time.

Effective and caring cross-cultural listening is essential. This is a real skill, hampered by stereotypes, expectations, judgmentalism, confusions about our "truths" and the validity of experience, and limited respect for the other person.

The intercultural differences among us are important and must be recognized and accepted on the way to discovering our commonalities. Starting out with "we're all human beings," or "I never notice a person's color," or "People are all basically the same" is a subtle form of racism because it denies our diverse cultural/personal experience and assumes that everyone is "just like me." The sense of unity and shared experience comes later.

Mutual respect, for one's own self and for the others is essential and the only basis on which intercultural relations have validity.

The environment in which we live (see #2) demands cultural assimilation, uniformity, coercion. It tends to denigrate cultural diversity, creates low self-esteem in minority groups, and leads to conflict, mistrust, oppression, and violence—both between the cultures and within the minority groups. It denies the richness of our varied cultural heritages and the things we can learn from each other.

Santa Fe Anglos, particularly newcomers, are often stereotyped as representatives of the legacy of cultural oppression regardless of their individual attitudes. Anger at the system is not necessarily directed at particular individuals. But most of the local minority people feel little reason to welcome or to voluntarily relate to Anglo newcomers.

Therefore, caring Anglos have to take the initiative, reaching out to make contacts, to learn, to share and to relate in whichever ways they can, and to remember that only time and involvement create trust and credibility. Mere "proximity" does not change hearts. But personal interactions can help break down stereotypes. Honesty and openness in sharing our stories can help create positive relationships.

Minority people, from necessity, learn to live in two worlds. Anglo people, generally, do not, and they often feel uncomfortable moving into other-culture environments. It's essential to reach out and risk such cultural discomfort in order to transcend it.

Minority people seldom go to intercultural gatherings or workshops for the sake of harmony, intelligent curiosity or getting acquainted. But they are interested in coming together to change conditions that create problems, to seek economic and social justice, to fight oppression, exploitation and racism that affect their communities.

❖ ❖ ❖

Vecinos Quiz

What is the Treaty of Guadalupe Hidalgo, and why is it still important?
Who was Popé? Why and how is he remembered?
When did commerce along the Santa Fe Trail begin, and why then?
What did the Bursum Bill threaten to destroy? How?
What was (is) the Black Legend?
What was the result of the Battle of Glorieta?
NAGPRA: what is it? Why is it important?
What is the official name of Santa Fe?
Stereotypes: when are they useful? When do they hurt?
What did the Laws of the Indies do?
The symbols of authority of the Pueblo governors: what are they?
What are Land Grants, and why are they still important?
What does *Vecinos* mean? In what sense?
What are "bug words"?
Why were artists so important in forming our tricultural Santa Fe?
What varieties of racism do you consider most lethal? Why?
Why are so many Hispanic kids school dropouts?
What do Anglos bring to our multicultural Santa Fe?
What is "stereotype smashing"?
How can caring individuals help defuse conflict situations?

❖ ❖ ❖

El Low-Rider
Mechanical and Cultural Shocks and Springs
    —Antonio E. Chavez, November 7, 1976

If we had only stopped to think deeply about the obvious,
while we sucked beer at the park

and watched him slowly circle the area,
his "loads"—twin pipes—rapping and moaning low.

We didn't notice, as his low-slung "ramfla" drew sparks
from the uneven pavement
that he was, unknowingly, trying to encourage
the rest of us to more prominence
in this non-ethnic, non-Chicano America!

Most of us missed the message
because we couldn't decipher it.
Only a few of his *raza* have appreciated him,
especially during the early years,
and even his admirers did not perceive
his full meaning and importance
to the Chicano community.

I estimate that the Chicano Low-Rider
has been cruising around since the early fifties,
maybe before then.
And the majority of us, his "proper" kin,
tried to ignore him or put him down.
We must have done those things because
we didn't understand who he really was
nor what he was trying to do.

This was terribly ironic because
we didn't know who we were nor
what we could do for our own personal reconciliation.
Yet we,
the high school finishers,
the college prep *vatos*,
found it easy not to respect our cousin:
the Chicano Low-Rider.

We should have joined him.
Then we could have learned from him
not only the art of altering the chassis,
springs, shock-absorbers and other mechanics:
but also courage that came the hard way;
where nightsticks, hate-stares and racial discrimination
were not as invisible nor as subtle
as on our high school campuses.
We could have learned to make a stand.
But look at us.

Look at us,
in the first and possibly the most abrasive and injurious environment we,
Chicanos, Blacks and Native Americans,
have had to contend with.
The school
stole the brightness from our eyes,
mangled our self-esteem,
fabricated weaknesses we didn't have
and enlarged those lies
until many of us dropped out in the eighth grade.

The educational system still
renders us mute and numbs us into feeling like
unwanted, problematic school furniture.
The school too often succeeds in making us believe
that we have nothing to be proud of.

Even the Chicanos going to college don't escape.
The collegiate are still quiet and hardly ever raise their hands
to signal academic success and self-confidence.
You can hear us say,
in the confidence of a Chicano "relief circle,"
"I knew the answer, *pero* I was afraid . . ."

And we regret our past scholastic forfeits because
those remembrances *desgraciadas* still haunt and burn within us,
the college graduates.
These memories still are painful because we know
we did nothing
to alleviate our collective burden between classes or after school.
More reason why we should have called upon
our outlaw *primo.*

We should have become closer with him because
although he dropped out of school,
a chicken-shit deal for him,
only the Low-Rider did something in rebellion.
Something rebellious which he thinly disguised
in iron and chrome.
The Low-Rider refused to obey
America's order of silence.
He took a many tonned monster from General Motors,
which conformed to Americano preferences,
and created an
artistic, cultural and mobile sculpture of defiance
with his Chicano Low-Rider.

With his singular creation, he changed
the most representative product of Americano society,
the automobile,
to meet his needs.
He converted the standard, all-American sacred-cow
into a Chicano enterprise.
And he accomplished this cultural tailoring
without hatred
but with enduring *cariño* and imagination,
to further perplex the non-ally.

Instead of accepting the cold Detroit engineering on the outside
and sterility on the inside,
the Low-Rider made his car
hug the road tightly,
sacrificing, perhaps mockingly, the Americano need
for speed and mechanical efficiency.
And the *vato* warmed the inside with redeeming images
of Saint Christopher or La Virgen de Guadalupe,
a nodding plastic dog,
a furry carpet on the dashboard,
a Chicano flag,
Mexican music
and other Chicano accouterments.

He must have done an outstanding job!
He is stopped often,
more often than a non-tattooed Chicano
driving a Volkswagen, a Bronco or a stock Chevy, by *La Chota,*
protector of the dominant society.
He is stopped for
having his license plate too close to the asphalt,
for driving too slow
and other trivial infractions.

The felonies are still being committed
by the Americanos on the pretext that
our cousin is a menace.
They imply that he is
too different, too distinctive, too difficult
to keep mute.
The main reason is that the Americano is afraid
of the Low-Rider's cruising signal of self-worth.

And I'm hoping that it's not too late for me to ride.

✤ ✤ ✤

Ten Commandments Of (Intercultural) Leadership

1. People are illogical, unreasonable and self-centered. Love and trust them anyway.
2. If you do good, people will accuse you of selfish ulterior motives. Do good anyway.
3. If you are successful, you will win some false friends and true enemies. Succeed anyway.
4. The good you do today will be forgotten tomorrow. Do good anyway.
5. Honesty and frankness will make you vulnerable. Be honest and frank anyway.
6. The biggest people with the biggest ideas can be shot down by the smallest people with the smallest ideas. Think big anyway.
7. People favor underdogs, but follow top dogs. Fight for the underdogs anyway.
8. What you spend years building may be destroyed overnight. Build anyway.
9. People really need help, but may attack you if you do help. Help people anyway.
10. Give the world the best you have and you may get kicked in the teeth. Give the world the best you have anyway.

—Author Unknown

For the Reader:

I hope you found the "tips" on these pages useful. They can be useful for consideration in discussion groups, or in sharing perspectives with others. Feel free to write your cmments in the margins.

As I wrote in the beginning, my hope is that these pages may help increase your awareness, comfort and effectiveness in your intercultural relationships, and may lead to warm enriching friendships for many years.

www.ingramcontent.com/pod-product-compliance
Lightning Source LLC
Chambersburg PA
CBHW031434270326
41930CB00007B/697